TEXAS'

BIG BEND COUNTRY

TEXT AND PHOTOGRAPHY BY GEORGE WUERTHNER

AMERICAN GEOGRAPHIC PUBLISHING

William A. Cordingley, Chairman
Rick Graetz, Publisher & CEO
Mark O. Thompson, Director of Publications
Barbara Fifer, Production Manager

ABOUT THE AUTHOR

Writer-photographer-naturalist George Wuerthner has been employed as a university instructor in California, a surveyor in Wyoming, a wilderness ranger in Alaska and a botanist in Idaho. He has backpacked, skied, kayaked and canoed extensively in wild places from Mexico to Alaska. His writing and photography have appeared in many natural history and outdoor publications and he has written several American Geographic Publishing titles.

American Geographic Publishing is a corporation for publishing illustrated geographic information and guides. It is not associated with American Geographical Society. It has no commercial or legal relationship to and should not be confused with any other company, society or group using the words geographic or geographical in its name or its publications.

ISBN 0-938314-64-5

© 1989 American Geographic Publishing
P.O. Box 5630, Helena, MT 59604
(406) 443-2842

Text © 1989 George Wuerthner
Design by Linda Collins
Printed in Korea by Dong-A Printing through Codra Enterprises, Torrance, CA

ACKNOWLEDGMENTS

In writing this book, I was assisted by many people and agencies. Although I cannot begin to name each person who provided information or insights, I thank them all. At Big Bend National Park, Ray Skiles and Mike Fleming were especially helpful by making Park Service files available to me. Rich LoBello of the Big Bend Natural History Association generously read an early draft of the manuscript.

Dick and Barb Baldwin helped with shuttles during river trips. In addition, they cheerfully made their travel trailer available as a home away from home and provided enjoyable company during part of my time in Big Bend.

I also was assisted by the library staff at Sul Ross University, who allowed me to review historical books and reports housed in their Big Bend Archives collection. The U.S. Fish and Wildlife Service, the Texas Parks and Wildlife Department, as well as the Chambers of Commerce in Marfa and Alpine all supplied information and background literature.

I read many books and papers by other authors that provided data and helpful interpretations of the many aspects of Big Bend's human and natural history. The papers are too numerous to list, but for readers who want a more in-depth treatment of any particular subject areas I would suggest the following books.

For a good overview of birds in Big Bend, try *A Field Guide to Birds of the Big Bend* by Roland Wauer. And, by the same author, a good introduction to common trees, birds, mammals, etc., is *Naturalist's Big Bend*.

For a very complete history nothing is better than *The Big Bend—A History of the Last Texas Frontier* by Ronnie Tyler, published by the National Park Service. For a less exhaustive history, see *Big Bend Country* by former park superintendent Ross Maxwell.

A somewhat outdated but nevertheless interesting look at the region's geological history can be gained from Ross Maxwell's *The Big Bend of the Rio Grande—A Guide to the Rocks, Landscape, Geologic History and Settlers of the Areas of Big Bend National Park*.

A wonderful botanical overview of the area is found in *Trees and Shrubs of Trans-Pecos Texas* by Michael Powell.

Finally, the single best book I found on natural history as well as ecological insights, although not exclusively focused on Big Bend, is Frederick Gehlbach's *Mountain Islands and Desert Seas—A Natural History of the U.S.-Mexican Borderlands*. To all the above authors, I, of course, owe thanks.

While I relied upon the National Park Service, university staff, and others for background material, the ideas, opinions and interpretations of data in this book are my own and in no way reflect the opinions of those who provided information.

Right: Park Service packer Mark Spurlock in Big Bend National Park.
Above: Sunset over Deadhorse Mountains.

To Alpine Gap

To Marathon

SANTIAGO MOUNTAINS

Persimmon Gap

PRIVATE LAND

Maravillas Canyon

RIO GRANDE WILD & SCENIC RIVER

Horse Canyon

State Hwy. 118

U.S. Hwy. 385

DAGGER FLAT

ROSILLOS MOUNTAINS

PRIVATE LAND

BLACK GAR WILDLIFE MANAGEMENT AREA

La Linda

Terlingua Cr.

Christmas Mountains

TORNILLO FLAT

BIG BEND RANCH STATE PARK

Willow Mtn.

Paint Gap Hills

Grapevine Hills

Old Ore Rd.

Stillwell Crossing

Panther Canyon

Fresno Cr.

Terlingua

Study Butte

PARK HEADQUARTERS

Ernst Tinaja

DEADHORSE MOUNTAINS

To Presidio

Lajitas

Big Hill

MESA DE ANGUILA

Rattlesnake Mtn.

Terlingua Abaja

BURRO MESA

Tule Mtn.

Ross Maxwell Scenic Dr.

The Window

The Basin

Boot Canyon

Panther Pk.

Dugout Wells

Emory Pk.

Lost Mine Pk.

Pine Canyon

Rio Grande Village

Boquillas Canyon

Sotol Vista Overlook

Blue Cr. Canyon

CHISOS MOUNTAINS

Hot Springs

Boquillas, Mexico

Santa Elena Canyon

Goat Mtn.

Sierra Quemada

Glenn Spring

Cerro Castellan

Mule Ears Peak

Elephant Tusk

Castolon

Dominguez Mtn.

Talley Mtn.

River Road

Mariscal Mine

Presidio de San Vicente (abdn.)

SIERRA DEL CARMEN

Punta de la Sierra

Black Dike

MARISCAL MOUNTAIN

Johnson Ranch

Rio Grande R.

Mariscal Canyon

SIERRA DE SAN VICENTE

MAP BY LINDA COLLINS BASED ON SHADED-RELIEF ART BY NATIONAL PARK SERVICE STAFF ARTIST BILL VON ALLMEN

CONTENTS

Left: Agave and the South Rim, Chisos Mountains.

Front cover: The view from Hot Springs Canyon across the Rio Grande toward the Sierra San Vicente.

Back cover, left: Agave.
Right: The Rio Grande at Boquillas Canyon.

Title page: "The Window" in the Chisos Mountains.

Page 2: Ocotillo above the Rio Grande at the mouth of Santa Elena Canyon.

DESERT AND MOUNTAINS

Above: Agave in Pine Canyon.

Facing page: The Rio Grande where it flows through the Sierra Del Carmen. Not until 1899 did anyone successfully float all the canyons of the Rio Grande, and until recently this area easily was one of the most remote parts of the lower 48 states.

Big Bend country. It still is one of the last frontiers in the lower 48 states. It is a land so empty that the Spanish dubbed it the *despoblado* or uninhabited land.

Even today, the Big Bend country is lightly populated. Within an area the size of Maryland live only 13,000 people, most residing in three towns: Alpine, the largest community with an estimated population of 6,575; Marfa, with 2,984 people; and Marathon, with fewer than a thousand people. El Paso, the closest metropolitan area, lies 320 miles northwest.

Big Bend country is the kind of place where you can drive a hundred miles of highway and watch the scenery and wildlife instead of having to watch the bumper of the car in front of you. The lack of industry, coupled with the arid climate, makes for exceptionally clear air—one reason the University of Texas has located McDonald Observatory atop Mount Locke in the nearby Davis Mountains.

The name Big Bend is derived from the looping course of the Rio Grande, which forms the border between Mexico and the United States. Trapped by a succession of magnificent canyons, the river twists its way first southeast and then northeast through the area. This is the "Big Bend." Big Bend National Park occupies its southernmost tip.

This book focuses on Big Bend National Park, but includes the slightly larger area bounded by Highway 67 between Presidio and Marfa on the west, Highway 90 from Marfa to Langtry on the north, and the Rio Grande on the southern border.

Although this entire region is often referred to as the Big Bend, the term most often brings to mind the national park. To those who know something about how most national parks were established, it is somewhat surprising that a national park is here at all.

Texas existed as a separate republic, not a territory, prior to its becoming a state. It therefore entered the Union with no major federal land holdings. As result, unlike other western states where the federal government retained ownership of unappropriated lands and could create national parks out of public domain, establishment of a national park in Texas required acquiring private land holdings. Beginning in the 1930s, the state of Texas began acquiring property in the Big Bend area for a park. In 1942, the state deeded some 708,221 acres to the federal government for a national park. However, the park was not officially created until 1944. Big Bend acreage remained the same until recently when, in 1987, the first major expansion was approved. Congress authorized the federal government to acquire the 67,125-acre Harte Ranch, which borders 15 miles of the park near Persimmon Gap. The ranch includes about half the Rosillos Mountains.

Since its creation, visitation to Big Bend has steadily increased and the national park is a centerpiece of the

Big Bend country tourist economy. When the park was established in 1944, there were just 1,409 visitors. By 1976, a record 456,200 people came to visit Big Bend. Since that time, numbers have dropped and only 274,921 people came in 1987 and 241,959 in 1988. The peak visitation is during the winter months, with the highest level in March. Certainly one reason for its winter popularity is the generally mild climate and abundant sunshine at this time of year.

Far and away most people merely drive the roads and take short hikes, but there has been increasing use of the back country. In particular, float trips down the Rio Grande through the magnificent canyons—Santa Elena, Mariscal and Boquillas—are growing in popularity. Some 191 miles of the river now are designated "Wild and Scenic" under the federal Wild and Scenic Rivers Act, which precludes dam construction, among other things. The designated stretch starts in Mariscal Canyon and extends in the park through Boquillas Canyon. It continues beyond the park borders to include what are known as the lower Rio Grande Canyons all the way to the Terrell-Val Verde County line near Langtry.

Within the park are a number of outstanding scenic and natural features including the Chisos Mountains— the only mountain range entirely within a national park. Emory Peak, at 7,835 feet, is the third-highest summit in Texas. The Chisos are also the southernmost mountain range in the United States, lying at about the same latitude as the mouth of the Mississippi River.

The Big Bend country is dominated by basin-and-range topography, with most mountain ranges trending northwest-southeast, separated by wide intervening

Left: From the top of Mt. Emory, highest peak in the Chisos Mountains, the third-highest range in Texas. Named for William Emory, head of U.S. Boundary Survey in 1850.
Facing page: Precipitation is higher in the Chisos Mountains than in the nearby valleys, and the highest peaks receive 25 or more inches per year.

basins drained by the Rio Grande and its tributaries. The Chisos form one of many ranges that rise from the West Texas plains. Outside the park are several major mountain ranges, including the Davis Mountains north of Alpine (whose highest peak is Mount Livermore at 8,382 feet) and the Chinati Mountains near Presidio, where Chinati Peak reaches an elevation of 7,730 feet. Other nearby mountain ranges include the Rosillos, Glass, Christmas, Bofecillos and Del Norte mountains.

Chihuahuan desert climate means summer moisture comes primarily as monsoonal thundershowers

———☆———

These mountain uplands can be grouped into two major types of rocks—igneous (volcanic) or sedimentary. In Big Bend, the Mesa de Anguila, Mariscal Mountain, Deadhorse Mountains and Santiago Mountains are all of sedimentary origin—primarily limestone. Other sedimentary mountains outside the park include the Glass and Del Norte mountains. The Chisos Mountains in Big Bend are of igneous origins, as are the nearby Bofecillos Mountains between Lajitas and Presidio, the Chinati Mountains and the Davis Mountains by Alpine.

The entire Big Bend region is considered part of the Chihuahuan Desert, one of four major desert regions in North America. The Chihuahuan is a relatively young desert, evolving since the last Ice Age ended and the climate warmed approximately 8,000 years ago. Only a small portion of this desert extends into the United States, primarily in southern New Mexico and West Texas. More than two thirds of the Chihuahuan desert lies in Mexico, in the states of Durango, Nuevo Leon, San Luis Potosí, Zacatecas, Chihuahua and Coahuila, within an intermountain plateau between the Sierra

Madre Oriental and the Sierra Madre Occidental. More than half this desert is above 4,000 feet elevation, making it the highest and best "watered" desert in North America. Because of its generally high elevation, winter temperatures often dip below freezing. Fort Davis once even recorded a temperature of 10° below zero. Summer temperatures are usually cooler than those of the nearby Sonoran Desert, although Presidio, north and west of Big Bend National Park, once recorded a temperature of 119°. This level is not characteristic of the Chihuahuan desert as a whole, but the area along the Rio Grande represents the lowest, hottest and driest portion of this desert.

The Chihuahuan desert climate is characterized by winter drought, with summer moisture coming primarily as monsoonal thundershowers. In fact, nearly 80 percent of its precipitation, derived from Gulf of Mexico air masses, falls during summer—peaking in July and August. February and March are the driest months.

Any generalities about temperature or precipitation must be considered along with elevation. Within Big Bend National Park elevations range from 1,800 feet at Stillwell Crossing on the Rio Grande, to 7,835 feet at Emory Peak in the Chisos Mountains, and annual precipitation and temperature vary tremendously with it. At relatively low elevation, Rio Grande Village records only slightly more than 10 inches of precipitation a year, while 3,000 feet higher in the Chisos Basin nearly 16 to 18 inches is the norm. The driest portion of the park—between Castolon and Mariscal Mountain—receives only five inches of precipitation a year,

Right: Lechuguilla, a plant found nowhere but the Chihuahuan Desert.

Facing page: The Rio Grande in Boquillas Canyon, the longest of the river's three major canyons within the national park—but the easiest to float.

while the highest mountaintops receive a distinctly un–desert-like precipitation of 20 to 25 inches annually.

But precipitation is not the only factor that defines a desert. Fort Yukon, Alaska has an annual precipitation of seven inches, yet few people who have slogged across the mosquito-infested muskeg there would call it a desert. The difference between central Alaska and West Texas is temperature and evapotranspiration. The hotter air temperatures of Texas result in far higher evaporation rates than occur in Alaska. Thus, for every inch of precipitation received, the actual moisture availability for plants and animals is much less in West Texas.

The climatic characteristics of each of the four major North American deserts influence what kinds of plants and animals typically inhabit each one. For example, the relatively cold Great Basin desert (Nevada and Utah) is dominated by sagebrush and has few succulents and cacti, both of which tend to be cold-sensitive. The Chihuahuan desert, with its summer rainfall, tends to be dominated by summer-blooming flowers, compared to the Mojave desert (southern California) with its winter rains. And, although cacti are far more abundant in the Chichuahuan desert than in the Great Basin desert, you will not see large columnar cacti species like the saguaro and caldron—which are synonymous with the Sonoran desert of Arizona and northern Mexico. But it is too cold here in Big Bend for such giant, frost-sensitive cactus. However, the diversity of prickly pear and hedgehog cacti is impressive. More than 70 cactus species have been recorded in Big Bend National Park alone.

The truly distinctive feature of the Chihuahuan desert is the abundance of succulents, including agaves and yuccas. One of the most characteristic of these is the

Left: Prickly pear cactus frames Pummel Peak in the Chisos Mountains.

Facing page: Hedgehog cactus along the Rio Grande near Hot Springs Canyon.

13

lechuguilla, typically found growing on limestone hills. Once you recognize it, you are not apt to forget the lechuguilla—it looks like bunches of bananas armed with dagger points. One does not walk carelessly through a hillside of lechuguilla! Other characteristic plants include tarbrush, creosote bush, ocotillo and a variety of yuccas.

Although the lowlands are desert, the park's higher elevations support woodlands more typical of forests farther north. These islands of northern habitat amidst desert lowlands account for some of the incredible diversity of Big Bend's flora and fauna. A number of plants and animals found here are rare or extinct elsewhere. However, Big Bend is not isolated from many of the forces that have eliminated species elsewhere, and 21 species are listed as endangered or threatened within Big Bend National Park—and another 20 soon may be added to the list. Some of these are relatively well known species, like the black bear and peregrine falcon, while others like the Chihuahua shiner or Big Bend mosquitofish are not familiar to most people.

This diversity of scenic and biological attributes is one reason Big Bend National Park was selected by the United Nations as a World Biosphere Reserve. The Biosphere Reserve system is designed to protect characteristic ecosystems of the world.

The importance of Big Bend National Park as a preserve may become increasingly important in future years as development in the region progresses. Communities bordering the park, like Study Butte and Lajitas, rapidly are becoming supply hubs for tourists and attractions in their own right. When I first visited Lajitas years ago, it was merely a trading post by the river. The post is still there but, in addition, condos

Left: Kayaking Rock Slide Rapid.

Facing page: Ocotillo in Santa Elena Canyon.

flourish, along with an RV park, a hotel, restaurant, shops and the newly established Lajitas Museum and Desert Garden. While some of these are tastefully designed, rampant development can affect scarce resources, like ground water. Nevertheless, properly planned tourist development is probably one of the more benign forms of economic development and tourism no doubt will become increasingly important for the regional economy.

Big Bend's diversity of scenic and biological attributes is one reason the United Nations selected it as a World Biosphere Reserve.

———— ☆ ————

The area's larger communities also depend economically on their healthful climates. Alpine and Marfa are both located at elevations in excess of 4,000 feet. Marfa, at 4,688 feet, likes to boast that it has the highest golf course in Texas. The relatively high elevation, an average precipitation of nearly 16 inches, and frequent sunshine, make these communities particularly attractive for retirement living.

Retirees and tourists, coupled with agriculture, make the communities of Alpine, Marfa and Marathon regional trade and service centers. Alpine also has Sul Ross University. The university's 2,200 students provide jobs for 600 employees. The next largest employer in Brewster County, which includes Big Bend National Park, is the federal government, with 143 employees.

While the park is the centerpiece for the region, the state of Texas recently acquired the Big Bend Ranch, which stretches from Lajitas to Presidio. The 215,000-acre ranch includes most of the spectacular and rugged Bofecillos Mountains and will be operated as a state

15

park. The state also owns the 112,638-acre Black Gap Wildlife Management Area, which includes frontage on the Rio Grande from La Linda to Reagan Canyon. Together these state and federal holdings constitute the largest parcels of public lands in Texas.

Recently, the idea of expanding federal ownership in the region by creating a Davis Mountain National Park has revived. The National Park Service studied the area 20 years ago. As some of the larger private ranches have been subdivided into small tracts for second homes, interest has arisen in preserving a large portion of these mountains in their natural condition. At present, however, short-sighted local opposition is aligned against such a proposal.

The Big Bend country is a land rich in history, scenic splendor and biological diversity. It genuinely deserves its reputation as the "best of Texas."

Left: Lower Canyons of the Rio Grande within the Wild and Scenic River section. This part of the river is more remote and less-often floated. It also is outside Big Bend National Park, although the Park Service has management authority for the Wild and Scenic segment.

Facing page: Sunset on Vernon Bailey Peak in the Chisos.

PEOPLE IN AN "UNINHABITED" LAND

Above: The graveyard at Terlingua.

Facing page: Moonset at sunrise over the Chisos Mountains.

The Big Bend country is a place bypassed by the major events of history. And its own history is sketchy at best. Nonetheless, echoes of the world at large reverberate everywhere in Big Bend's past.

First humans

Evidence of human occupation in the Big Bend region dates from the closing days of the Ice Age some 10,000 years ago. At that time, the regional climate was wetter and cooler and woodlands dominated many areas that are now desert. Wooly mammoth, camel, giant bison and other large Ice Age mammals were common. About 10,000 to 9000 B.C., human hunters entered the region, presumably from the north. These paleo-Indians, as they are called, were primarily big-game hunters. Lacking the bow and arrow, nets, boats and other inventions to come later, these Indians were nevertheless effective hunters of the late Pleistocene (Ice Age) fauna. Some scientists even have speculated that they may have contributed to the extinction of many Ice Age mammals.

By 8000 to 6000 B.C. the regional climate had become warmer and drier. The Chihuahuan Desert is said to have evolved at this time. With the extinction of Ice Age mammals, the indigenous people adopted a lifestyle less dependent upon hunting, one utilizing more plant resources. Archaeological evidence is scanty compared to that of other regions, but this may be because few archaeological investigations have been carried out here.

But evidence of human occupation by the Middle Archaic age (3000-500 B.C.) is widespread. Although the climate was generally arid, sometime between 2000 and 500 B.C. moisture increased, so that bison—and hence bison hunters—occasionally entered the Trans-Pecos region. However, no evidence suggests that bison were actually in Big Bend country.

Adapted to a nomadic existence dependent upon small game and a variety of plants such as mesquite beans, prickly pear cactus, yucca blossoms and century plant, most of the early Indians located their activities around springs and in caves and rock shelters where grinding slabs, scraping tools, sandals, basketry and other artifacts have been found. Most sites are in the foothills and basins, although people occasionally used the mountains as well.

Between 500 B.C. and 1500 A.D., Southwestern Indian lifestyle changed profoundly. Pottery making and agriculture were introduced from Mexico and began to spread throughout the region. This changed the hunter-gatherer, nomadic life to one centered on crops and seasonal camps, if not semi-permanent villages, established in fertile floodplains of rivers such as the Rio Grande. By 1200 A.D. (about the time of the Middle Ages in Europe), pithouse villages were located as far south as Presidio and Redford. Not all

18

Indians turned to agriculture, however, and in what is now Big Bend, Indians still retained their old hunter-gatherer life ways. This group as well as others eventually benefited from a third technological innovation—the bow and arrow. It is only within the last thousand years that Indians of the Big Bend region adopted this weapon. Prior to this time, throwing-spears were their only arms. The bow and arrow increased efficiency and reduced the risk associated with hunting big game.

The Spanish era

Changes for the Indians began to come much more rapidly than in the past. Just 43 years after Columbus first encountered the New World, a Spanish soldier, Cabeza de Vaca, is believed to have entered the Big Bend region. De Vaca was shipwrecked on the Texas Coast in 1528, where he was held captive by Indians for seven years. He eventually escaped and began working his way across Texas to Mexico. Although his exact route is subject to interpretation, most historians believe De Vaca was guided by Indians to a crossing on the Rio Grande by present-day Presidio, which he reached in 1535. Here De Vaca found villages where the inhabitants grew beans, corn and pumpkins. The explorer commented that a tribe to the north regularly traveled to the northeast to hunt "cattle"—probably a reference to bison common on the grasslands about the Pecos River.

These pueblo-dwelling Indians, known as the Jumanos, as well as the nomadic hunting tribes that wandered in the Davis and Chisos mountains, spoke a Uto-Aztecan language. They are linked linguistically with the Shoshonean-speaking groups of the Great Basin, as well as the Indians dwelling in northern Mexico. The village-dwelling group De Vaca met

Left: Mouth of Santa Elena Canyon.

Facing page: *Juniper Canyon seen from Lost Mine Trail.*

was likely one of the farthest outposts of the Pueblo Indians whose ruins are common in New Mexico, Arizona and southern Utah. Like the groups farther north, the Indians living on the Rio Grande appeared to be declining in prosperity when De Vaca reached them.

It was 46 years later, in 1581, when the next Spanish party entered the region. A group of Franciscan friars under the leadership of Fray Agustin Rodriguez ventured from the mining settlement of Bartolome in northern Mexico and traveled down the Rio Conchos to its confluence with the Rio Grande near present-day Presidio. Here, Rodriguez found the same Indian villages De Vaca had seen, and which the Spanish later referred to as La Junta (the Junction) because they sat at the confluence of the Rio Conchos and Rio Grande. From here Rodriguez turned northward, following the Rio Grande into New Mexico.

Just a year after the Rodriguez party had passed down the Rio Conchos, another Spanish adventurer, Antonio de Espejo, followed the Conchos to its confluence with the Rio Grande and continued northeast to the Pecos River. He named it Rio de las Vacas, or River of the Cows, for the many bison in that vicinity. With Jumanos Indians as guides, De Espejo eventually returned to the Rio Conchos villages via an Indian trail which in all likelihood followed Alamito Creek down to the Rio Grande near Presidio.

After a new route to the Spanish settlements in New Mexico was established via El Paso, traffic down the Rio Conchos dwindled. Occasionally, the Spanish would foray into the region to capture Indians to be sold as slaves to mine operators in Mexico, and a few missionary expeditions came and went. But for the most part, Indians living in the Big Bend region were largely ignored, although Spanish conquests were taking their toll on indigenous people to the north.

The encroaching Spanish frontier in northern Mexico made an enticing target for the more nomadic

Indians of the Big Bend area, including the Chisos. By the late 1600s, the aggressive Apaches invaded the Big Bend region, displacing the Chisos and other Indians. The Mescalero Apaches were an Athabascan-speaking tribe related to the Navajo, and had drifted down from Northwest Canada and moved into the Big Bend region after being evicted from lands farther north by the Comanches and Utes. The Apaches established small farms in New Mexico where they raised crops during the growing season, while raiding Spanish settlements during the remainder of the year. However, continuous attack from the Comanches eventually forced the Apaches farther south into the dry, rugged, uninhabited land of the Big Bend region, *despoblado* to the Spanish.

For the Apaches, the despoblado became both home and sanctuary. They adapted to the harsh, dry land, learning what could be eaten and where the waterholes were, and occasionally growing crops on small rancherias in the Chisos and other mountains. However, given the overall low productivity of the land, it was the continuous supply of livestock, horses and slaves captured during frequent raids into Mexico that may have allowed the Apache to survive here in much larger numbers than otherwise would have been possible. Traveling light, the Apaches made raid after raid into Mexico, then quickly retreated with their booty to the trackless wastes of the despoblado, where the Spanish were loath to follow.

In 1667 Governor Antonio de Oca Sarmiento of Nueva Vizcaya suggested that the Spanish set up a series of small forts or "presidios" to defend the northern frontier. The governor's suggestion was not acted upon for decades. In the meantime, the Coman-

Left: The Rio Grande near Boquillas Canyon.

Facing page: Blue Creek Canyon, among the undisputed strongholds of Apache people who raided frontier ranches and villages in Mexico from here.

ches obtained horses and soon ruled the southern Plains, including most of West Texas, Oklahoma and southeastern New Mexico. With their newfound mobility, the Comanches soon were raiding Mexican ranches and settlements as well. They made forays each September into Mexico during what came to be called the Comanche Moon.

So frequent were these raids that a trail as much as a mile wide, lined by the bleached bones of horses and cattle that had died during Comanche retreats from Mexico, marked this pathway to the frontier. The trail had two branches, one that led through what is now Big Bend National Park at Persimmon Gap northeast toward Marathon, while the other crossed the river at present-day Lajitas. They united near Marathon and continued to Comanche Spring (now Fort Stockton).

Although the Spanish sent several expeditions into the Rio Grande region during the early 1700s, none actually penetrated the area we now know as Big Bend National Park. As Indian depredations increased, the Spanish finally decided to implement the proposed presidio system. In 1747, an expedition was dispatched to the Rio Grande to locate presidio sites. It was led by the governor of Coahuila, Pedro de Rabago y Teran, who traveled from Chihuahua by a circular route that took him to the Rio Grande somewhere between present-day Rio Grande Village and Mariscal Canyon. Although his exact route is not known, some historians believe that Rabago became the first European to travel through what is now Big Bend National Park. Rabago is thought to have traveled up Terlingua Creek to avoid Santa Elena Canyon and then swung back to the river near present-day Lajitas, before finally making his way upriver to the pueblos at La Junta. On his return trip Rabago traveled around the north side of the Chisos then he turned south and crossed the Rio Grande near San Vicente. Rabago scouts reported finding several old Apache campsites in the Chisos Mountains.

Rabago recommended that a presidio be constructed at La Junta and, some 13 years after his expedition, Presidio del Norte was completed there. A second presidio was built at San Vicente in 1774 (two years prior to the American Revolution) to help discourage Indian raiding parties on the Comanche Trail, but was abandoned only a few years later.

Even though the Apache and Comanche were united in their hatred of the Spanish, they nevertheless were continuously at war with each other. The Spanish were able on occasion to exploit this mutual animosity by pledging to protect one group against attacks by the other. For example, in 1791, the Spaniards offered to protect the Apaches if they ceased attacks on frontier towns and ranches in exchange for protection against marauding Comanche.

The Spanish were responsible for much of the early exploration of the Big Bend region, but they had no interest in it other than for defense purposes. For them, it would always be the despoblado—the uninhabited land. It was the Anglo-Americans influence that soon would shape the destiny of the Big Bend country. By the early 1800s, events farther east that would profoundly change the Big Bend frontier were shaping up.

The Anglo-Americans

In 1821, the Provincial Governor of Texas signed an agreement with an American, Moses Austin, granting him permission to establish an Anglo colony in Spanish territory. When Moses died suddenly, the governor recognized Moses' son, Stephen, as heir to the grant. In 1822, however, Mexico gained independence from Spain and the legality of the grant was clouded. Austin traveled to Mexico City and pleaded

Right: Yuccas and Sierra del Carmen.

Facing page: Punta de la Sierra.

his case before the new government of Mexico, which not only recognized the grant, but modified it to include more generous terms. Within a year Austin had welcomed 1,800 people (including 443 slaves) to his Texas colony. Little did the Spanish know that they had opened a flood gate to Anglo-American immigration. By 1830 there were more than 20,000 Americans living in Texas and, as the Mexicans soon learned, most of these immigrants were opinionated, aggressive and haughty, with contempt for authority of any kind.

As the Mexican government attempted to clamp down on immigration, the Americans became more and more belligerent. Hostilities came to a head in 1835 when Stephen Austin successfully attacked the provincial capital of San Antonio. After routing the Mexicans, the Americans set up their own republic with Sam Houston in charge of forces. But in February of 1836, General Santa Anna and 4,000 troops attacked the provincial capital. A small American force holed up in an old mission that they renamed the Alamo. Santa Anna's troops stormed the mission, killing all 187 defenders, but the victory cost the general one third of his army. In addition, the heretofore loosely organized Americans rallied behind the cry "Remember the Alamo." Santa Anna later was captured and forced to sign a treaty that recognized Texas as an independent republic with the Rio Grande as its boundary. Big Bend was now under Anglo-American political control.

The new Republic of Texas had one valuable asset—land. And in 1836 the Texas Congress passed a law granting 1,280 acres to any family who settled in the republic. Between 1836 and 1846, the population

Left: Glenn Springs, where a candellia wax factory began in 1911. In 1916, an unknown number of Mexican bandits raided the community, killing four people.

Facing page: Lechugilla and Sierra del Carmen.

swelled from 30,000 to 140,000. Texas entered the Union as the 28th state in 1845, giving the U.S. government justification for policing its borders, including the long-isolated country surrounding the Big Bend. When the Treaty of Guadalupe Hidalgo was signed in 1848, the way was paved for American settlement of the Big Bend country.

One of the first American settlers was Ben Leaton who, along with John Spencer and John Burgess, purchased land for a trading post on the Rio Grande near Presidio. Leaton operated a successful business at least partially dependent upon Indian depredations into Mexico. Leaton would trade ammunition and guns to the Apache and Comanche in exchange for stolen livestock.

Under American control, trade increased between San Antonio and El Paso. With the 1849 discovery of gold in California, there was renewed interest in the San Antonio-El Paso route as thousands of gold seekers traveled by the snow-free southern route to the Pacific. En route, these travelers and traders crossed the major Indian trails leading into Mexico and many suffered at the hands of the Comanche and Apache.

In response, the U.S. government built Fort Davis in 1854, along with several other forts, which sliced the Indians' territory in half. Fort Davis provided not only limited protection to travelers on the trails, but also a market for livestock, thus encouraging the early ranching industry. One of the first individuals to take advantage of military contracts was John Spencer, one of Leaton's original partners. Spencer operated a ranch near Shafter.

Since travel concentrated on the major trails, much of the Big Bend country remained largely *terra incognita*. Although the Spanish had touched portions of the Rio Grande, no one had as yet explored the course of the Rio Grande from Presidio to Eagle Pass. The Treaty of Guadalupe Hidalgo required a

survey of the Mexican-U.S. border, a task assigned to Major William H. Emory. Between 1856 and 1857, Emory's men worked their way down through the rugged Big Bend country, and named a high, prominent peak in the Chisos Mountains for their commander. Emory Peak is not only the highest mountain in the Chisos, but the third-highest peak in Texas.

The going was tough, but Tyler Chandler, field leader of the Emory survey, still was impressed by the Big Bend scenery. After working through the Sierra Del Carmens, Chandler wrote, "No description can give an idea of the grandeur of the scenery through these mountains. There is no verdure to soften the bare and rugged view; no overhanging trees or green bushes to vary the scene from one of perfect desolation. Rocks are here piled one above another over which it was with the greatest labor that we would work our way."

The survey party had a boating mishap attempting to float through Santa Elena Canyon, but did successfully navigate Mariscal Canyon (although they lost one boat there, too). They detoured around Boquillas Canyon and, after crossing the Sierra Del Carmens with additional losses of mules and supplies, Chandler decided to give up on the rest of the survey. He, along with most of the party, headed overland to Fort Duncan near Eagle Pass. However, several men decided that they would rather take their chances on the river than risk Indian attack and thirst on the overland route. In the remaining boat, they floated to Eagle Pass—becoming the first whites to successfully navigate the lower canyons of the Rio Grande.

The first successful float through *all* the Rio Grande Canyons did not come until 1899, when a

Right: Juniper snag along Lost Mine Trail.

Facing page: Fort Davis was established in 1854 on the main trail between San Antonio and El Paso, its soldiers assigned to patrol the border and pacify the Apache and Comanche.

U.S. Geological Survey team led by Robert Hill ran the river from Presidio to Langtry. Equipped with cameras, Hill brought back some of the first pictures displaying the scenic beauty of the Rio Grande canyons, which would later lead to their inclusion in the park.

A few years after the Emory surveys, in 1859 and 1860, Lieutenant William Echol explored the Big Bend area with camels as part of an experiment testing the feasibility of using the beasts for military use. Echol left Fort Davis in July 1859, each camel loaded with 400 pounds of supplies and gear. (Most pack horses do not carry more than 200 pounds.) The camel expedition passed through Dog Canyon by Persimmon Gap and followed the Comanche Trail to the Rio Grande and then Echol returned to Fort Stockton. During the summer of 1860, Echol made a second successful camel trip into the Big Bend country. The camels had done admirably well. During one portion of their trip they had gone nearly five days without water and, overall, ate much less food than horses or mules. Despite their proven ability, camels never captured the imagination of the Americans and the idea of camel pack trains slowly faded into history. Two local mountains commemorate this unusual experiment: Camels Hump north of Study Butte along Highway 118, and Horse Mountain south of Marathon, sometimes called Camels Hump as well.

The hostile Indians of the Big Bend region were a major obstacle to settlement. Throughout the 1860s and 1870s, the Indians raided almost at will and the Army was powerless to stop them. For the Indian there were few other alternatives to raiding. The whites had moved into the better lands to the north and east, wiping out the herds of big game animals and replacing them with domestic livestock. Like the Mexican wolf, which was subdued only a few decades later than the Indian, they had nothing to eat but the settlers' livestock—there was no wildlife left. Texas'

Indian policy was characterized by the great Indian photographer Edward Curtis: "Go elsewhere or be exterminated."

The last major Indian threat came from the Apache chief, Victorio, and his band of 200 to 300 warriors who raided on both sides of the border until his death at the hands of Mexican troops in Chihuahua in 1880. With Chief Victorio gone, the Army was able to round up the last Indians and place them on reservations in New Mexico.

Early development

With the Indians pacified, the Trans-Pecos region was safe for settlement. But long distances from markets and poor transportation made commerce unprofitable. It took the railroad to make development of the Big Bend region economically feasible. In 1881-1882, tracks from the Texas and New Orleans Railroad circled the edge of the Davis Mountains, and small towns like Murphyville (later changed to Alpine), Marfa and Marathon sprang up along the right of way.

The first real industry to develop was ranching. Scattered livestock operations had existed for centuries, including the herds kept by the various Spanish presidios as well as those of traders like Ben Leaton. However, these were all relatively small herds that used very little of the region's potential pasturage. With the threat of Indian pillage gone and the railroad available for moving stock to market, big-time ranching developed rapidly.

The Big Bend region at first appeared a favorable

Right: Historic home of Gilberto Luna on the Old Maverick Road. Luna farmed the nearby wash and supposedly lived beyond 100 years.

Facing page: Mariscal Mine, whose quicksilver deposit was discovered in 1900. The mine operated until 1927 and was reopened temporarily during World War II.

place for raising livestock. The summers were tolerable, particularly in lands above 3,000 feet, and the winters were relatively mild. In places, grass was abundant, and springs, creeks and other water sources were, if not abundant, at least readily available.

The first big-time rancher was Milton Faver. His headquarters in the Chinati Mountains near Presidio resembled a small fort complete with gun ports and a small cannon. Faver's original herd of 300 Mexican cattle eventually grew to an estimated 10,000 to 20,000. Other ranchers raised sheep. George Crosson, who started a ranch near Fort Davis, reportedly had 10,000 sheep in 1882. James Gillett's G-4 ranch was organized in 1885. With headquarters on Terlingua Creek, the ranch included lands in what is now the western part of Big Bend Park. Beginning with 6,000 cattle in 1885, in six years the herds increased to almost 30,000 cattle. By 1886, the year of the first big roundup here, more than 60,000 head of cattle ranged the Big Bend region.

However, the ranchers were living on borrowed capital. The arid grasslands evolved without large grazing mammals and could not sustain such numbers without severe impact. The Big Bend region is a desert. Drought is not unusual, and the climate can be described as dry with an occasional wet year. In the late 1880s, the region suffered three dry years in a row. This was a normal occurrence for the region, but more optimistic locals called it a drought. The lack of rain meant little forage production, but cattle remained on the rangelands and the first widespread overgrazing of the Big Bend country occurred.

Early accounts support this contention. J.O.

Left: Hot Springs Post Office. J.O. Langford established his trading post and resort here in 1911.

Facing page: Terlingua Abaja, lower Terlingua Creek. Small farms sprouted on the floodplains of the area to feed miners in Terlingua.

Langford, who ran the Hot Springs Resort on the Rio Grande starting in the early 1900s, characterized Tornillo Flats by the present-day Fossil Exhibit as a verdant valley with waist-high grass. Early settlers cut hay there at one time. Today Tornillo Flat is a badland of eroded gullies and creosote flats.

Ranchers increased the number of sheep and goats, particularly during World War I. Overgrazing increased. The abused and depleted landscape could no longer support large numbers of animals, and by the 1930s ranching in what soon would become Big Bend National Park was a marginal proposition at best.

Mining began to boom in the Big Bend country about the same time that ranching was established and it benefited also from the simultaneous cessation of Indian raids and the coming of the railroad. One of Ben Leaton's partners, John Spencer, found silver ore in the Chinati Mountains, which ultimately led to the development of the Presidio Mine. Underground mining began in 1883 and continued off and on until 1942. At one time more than 300 men were employed in mining operations. During this long period of operation, more gold, lead and silver came out of this single mine than from any other in Texas.

Remains of another silver mine operation can be seen along the Ore Terminal Road by Boquillas Canyon. Silver, zinc and lead ore mined across the Rio Grande in Mexico was carried to the U.S. side via a six-mile-long tramway. Here it was loaded into wagons for the long haul to the railhead in Marathon.

Despite these few hard-rock mining success stories, the Big Bend region in general is not a good place for finding precious minerals. Although limited amounts of gold, silver and other metals were mined, the region is best known for its quicksilver or mercury production.

In 1884 the first quicksilver mining operation was begun by California Hill near Terlingua. This first

operation was not profitable, but it was enough to entice other prospectors into the area. In 1896 the Marfa and Mariposa Company was organized and from the same area extracted more than 9,000 flasks of mercury. At its height, 1,500 workers, most of them Mexican, were employed at the mine. In what would be considered slave labor today, men worked seven days a week, 10 hours a day, for a dollar to a dollar and a half per day!

Mining the ore was difficult. All work was done by hand. Picks and shovels broke up the rock, then men carried the ore up ladders in backpacks. After a crusher broke it into small pieces, the ore was cooked to vaporize the quicksilver. In a process something like that of a home-made still, the fumes were collected in pipes and then cooled, condensing the mercury into a liquid.

Fuel for the furnaces was difficult to obtain in this largely treeless area. Trees were cut and hauled to the mines from as far away as the Chisos Mountains and even Mexico. Coal was mined near Study Butte for a short time and used as an alternative to wood. After World War II, butane gas was used.

The success of the Marfa and Mariposa Mining Company encouraged development of other mines. The Chisos Mining Company, formed by Howard Perry (whose mansion still can be seen in Terlingua), began work in 1902. Thirty mines operated at one time or another within the 14-by-4-mile belt of mineralized rock. Texas became the number-two producer of mercury in the nation. Mining activity in the Terlingua mines fluctuated depending upon mercury prices, and the last operations occurred in the late 1960s.

The mining activity at Terlingua prompted development of other area prospects. The ruins of one of these, the Mariscal Mine, lie within Big Bend National Park on the north slope of Mariscal Mountain. The ore deposit, first discovered in 1900, was worked sporadically until 1927. An attempt to reopen the mine during World War II failed, and today the mine is one of Big Bend's historic sites.

A third local industry to develop just after the turn of the century was wax-making. Candelilla, a plant native only to the Chihuahuan desert, produces a protective wax to decrease water losses in the arid climate. The wax originally was used as sealing wax, but later it found its way into the manufacture of everything from phonograph records to chewing gum. Wax factories arose wherever the plant was abundant and water was available. Several factories were located within today's park, including large ones at McKinney Springs and Glenn Springs. In 1914 there were 40 to 60 Mexicans working at the Glenn Springs factory alone.

To produce the wax, the one- to two-foot-long gray-green stems of the candelilla plants are collected. Workers place these in large vats with a mixture of boiling water and sulfuric acid. The wax separates from the plant and floats to the surface to be skimmed off. Candelilla wax still is produced in Mexico, and river floaters on occasion will find small wax camps along the river.

Around the turn of the century, small farms were developed along the Rio Grande floodplain. For example, by the early 1900s several families were growing cotton and grains on the site of Rio Grande Village. Other farms, many operated by Mexican-

Right: Located just outside the park, Terlingua is a ghost town slowly being reclaimed. At one time, more than 30 mercury mines here employed mostly Mexican miners who worked for seven days a week at $1 a day.

Facing page, top: The Perry Mansion in Terlingua, reminder of when the town was home to more than 1,500 people.
Bottom: Terlingua Abaja. Adobe was the preferred material for home construction, lending coolness in summer and warmth in winter.

Americans, dotted the area around Castolon, and on Terlingua Creek, Tornillo Creek, Alamo Creek and Blue Creek.

Border troubles

Never a settled border area, the Big Bend region experienced increased unrest after the Mexican Revolution in 1911. Many banditos took advantage of the opportunity to steal horses and raid on both sides of the border, with little fear of retribution. In 1912, bandits raided the Mexican villages of Boquillas and San Vicente, just across the river from the present Big Bend National Park. And in 1913, these outlaws robbed two ranches near Alpine taking horses, guns and saddles. In 1916, near Alpine, several bandits were caught attempting to derail a train. And on May 5, 1916, approximately 80 bandits crossed the border and attacked Glenn Springs and Deemer's Store at Boquillas, Texas (present-day Rio Grande Village). Four soldiers stationed at Glenn Springs to patrol the border, were killed, as was seven-year-old Tommy Compton. Meanwhile, Deemer's store was looted and the store's owner, Jesse Deemer, and his clerk, Monroe Payne, were taken hostage. The outlaws took six more hostages from the American-run silver mines near Boquillas, Mexico and headed into Mexico.

The U.S. Army pursued the bandits across the border using both horses and cars. After 16 days of pursuit, some of the hostages had escaped, while the Army had managed to free several others. Many of the stolen supplies were recovered and several bandits were killed or captured.

Left: Piñon frames the Sierra Quemada.

Facing page, top: Steam engine at Castolon once pumped river water into the fields to support cotton crops. Today mesquite and other riparian plants have recolonized the fields.
Bottom: Castolon Ranger Station housed the Cartledge family cook after the never-occupied cavalry post was sold.

In response to the continued threat along the border, President Wilson called out the National Guard. By August 1916, 100,000 troops had been assembled along the international border. Some of the guardsmen assigned to patrol the Big Bend area admired the scenery and wrote home suggesting that the only thing the area was really good for was a national park, thereby broaching the topic of park establishment for the first time.

Despite the troops, several other raids occurred. The L.C. Brite Ranch near Marfa was raided on Christmas Day 1917, and several people were killed. The Texas Rangers pursued the outlaws into Mexico, and surrounded the bandits' alleged hide-out. A shoot-out followed, in which eight to 50 people (sources vary) were killed. Although the retaliation was supposed to discourage future raids, the Ed Nevill Ranch near Presidio was raided in March of 1918. Again, American forces crossed into Mexico and another battle ensued, in which a reported 32 bandits were killed.

In response to the continuing border troubles, the Army built Camp Santa Helena at Castolon in what is now the park. However, by the time the post was completed in 1920, the troubles had disappeared and the post was closed in 1921 and later bought and converted to a store and residence. It is now a park historic site.

Life was quiet on the border in the 1920s. Then the dry years of the 1930s came, along with the Depression. During this time, discussions recurred about the need for new state parks in West Texas. In 1933, two state representatives, E.E. Townsend from Alpine and R.M. Wagstaff from Abilene, introduced a bill in the Texas legislature that would establish a Texas Canyons State Park centered on the Rio Grande. The bill withdrew from sale state lands south of latitude 29°25' N in Brewster County and directed that they be considered for use in the proposed

parklands. Legislators added the Chisos Mountains and the changed the name to Big Bend State Park.

Creating the park

At the same time that the Texas legislature was moving towards establishing a park centered on the Rio Grande, the federal government had created the Civilian Conservation Corps (CCC). One of their first missions in Texas was to improve the newly-created park. By 1934, two CCC companies were working in the Basin area of the Chisos Mountains. One of their first projects was to improve the very rough road leading up Green Gulch into the Basin. This is the same route still used today. The CCC camp was deactivated in 1937.

That same year, legislators proposed that the state park be made a national park. Momentum for the idea grew quickly and the Texas State Legislature considered a bill appropriating $4,400,000 to purchase all the private holdings in the Big Bend region for a national park. The bill was amended several times but eventually defeated. This inspired a group of private citizens and organizations like the Alpine Chamber of Commerce to create the Big Bend National Park Association, which sought to raise funds for land acquisition.

In 1938, Texas elected a new governor, one more supportive of the national park idea. The governor, Lee O'Daniel, urged the legislature to provide funds for land acquisition and park establishment. Opposition remained strong enough that it was not until 1941 that a bill authorizing $1,500,000 for land acquisition and park establishment finally passed the Texas legislature and Governor O'Daniel signed it

Left: Ruins at Glenn Springs.

Facing page: *The Sierra del Carmen seen from Boquillas Canyon.*

into law. By the end of 1942, the state had purchased nearly 700,000 acres for the new national park.

However, just because a state legislature is willing to purchase land for a national park does not mean the federal government has to accept it. Therefore, the U.S. Congress also had to take up the Big Bend National Park proposal. A bill authorizing the federal government to accept lands deeded by the state of Texas and to create a Big Bend National Park had been passed by the House and Senate back in June 1935. The bill directed the Secretary of Interior to designate park boundaries within a 1,500,000-acre area in the Big Bend region of Texas. On June 12, 1944, Secretary of Interior Harold Ickes accepted title to the lands purchased by the state of Texas for the establishment of Big Bend National Park.

When the establishment of Big Bend National Park was first being discussed, the possibility of creating a sister park in Mexico had arisen. As early as 1935, a meeting to develop the international park idea had been held between representatives of the Republic of Mexico and National Park Service. Several other meetings took place during the late 1930s, and interest continued even during and after the disruption of World War II. But it remains unresolved. There still are supporters for an international park; however, as yet, Mexico never has designated a park in the Big Bend region.

If and when Mexico does designate a park, its boundaries likely will include the dramatic Sierra Del Carmen, which rises beyond Rio Grande Village, and the even higher Fronteriza Mountains farther south. These ranges are more than a thousand feet higher than the Chisos Mountains on the American side, hence are more forested and have wildflower meadows, more water and an abundance of wildlife.

A GEOLOGICAL PARK

Above: Fossils in limestone near Hot Springs.

Facing page: Mule Ears Peaks are the eroded remains of igneous sills and are prominent landmarks in the Big Bend country.

Big Bend is first and foremost a geological park. While Big Bend is the nation's best representation of the Chihuahuan Desert and its only national park on the Mexican border (and thus important for ecological and historical reasons), the park's scenic qualities—a direct manifestation of its geological history—are what prompted its establishment in 1944. Appropriately, Big Bend's first superintendent, Dr. Ross Maxwell, was a geologist.

A note of caution in regard to geology: there are no absolutes in this field. Geologists must piece together what happened millions of years ago from tiny fragments of evidence visible today. Erosion literally strips away a great deal of geological history, leaving physical gaps called "uncomformities," which are covered by subsequent soil deposition.

New research often demands new interpretations of past theories, which must be kept in mind when considering Big Bend's geology. In gross features, the geology explained today is the same as that described in the past: volcanic rock is still volcanic rock, limestone is still limestone. However, the interpretation of how rocks and features came to be has changed in the past, and probably will change—to some extent—in the future.

Two major rock types dominate Big Bend. The oldest rocks are sedimentary in origin, while most of the younger rocks are igneous (volcanic). Sedimentary rocks usually are formed by deposition of rock fragments and soil in oceans or lakes. In Big Bend, the Deadhorse Mountains, Sierra del Carmen, Mariscal Mountain, Santiago Mountains and Mesa de Anguila are composed of sedimentary rocks—mostly limestones, shales and sandstones.

Igneous rocks form from melted magma and can be extruded as lava, as in a volcanic eruption, or remain buried as intrusive rocks that we see only if erosion strips away the overlying mantle of cap rocks. Igneous rocks are very common in Big Bend and the Chisos Mountains are largely volcanic in origin.

The rocks record the geological changes that have shaped the landscape now known as the Big Bend country. The rock record of this region includes formations that were laid down as sediments in an ancient ocean nearly 300 million years ago. Yet the record is not complete. Large sections of Big Bend's geological history were eroded away, leaving missing gaps. Thus we have records of rocks laid down 300 million years ago, but of the period between 280 million years and 136 million years, there is no record. Piecing together a geological history from the remaining fragments includes a lot of conjecture, but there is a story to tell.

The greatest difficulty non-geologists have in comprehending Big Bend's geological history results from our perspective of time. We are accustomed to

thinking in terms of our own time scale: human lifetimes are a "long" time. However, to understand Big Bend's geological history, we need to change our perspective, and even the way we think about the "solid" rock beneath our feet. Even as you read this book, the ground beneath you is moving as if on a conveyor belt. However, this motion is so slow it cannot be detected except by sensitive machines. Huge chunks of the earth's crust, called "plates," are floating on a semi-liquid center of molten rock. Convection currents deep in the earth cause these fragments to wander slowly about the surface of the globe. Sometimes crustal plates are pulled apart, while at other times, they collide with each other. These collisions often drive up mountain ranges as is now occurring where the Indian subcontinent is driving into the Asian plate, creating the Himalayan Mountains in the process.

Ancient seas

The oldest exposed rocks in Big Bend are found near Persimmon Gap on the road to Marathon. These are more than 300 million years in age. At this time North America was attached to Europe and Asia and straddling the equator. The fossils in the rocks at Persimmon Gap include sponges, brachiopods and other marine animals that live in warm waters. At that time, lush swampy forests covered much of what would become the North American continent. Amphibians, unable to live without moisture at least some of the year, dominated the earth—the dinosaur was yet to evolve.

Right: Volcanic necks rising from ash flow near Cerro Castellan look like petrified trees, but formed when molten rock was intruded into the surrounding ash deposit and hardened in place. Later the softer ash eroded away.

Facing page: The Grapevine Hills are laccoliths, which occur when magma rises close to earth's surface and cools slowly in place; erosion later strips away overlying rock.

In this warm, moist climate, plant growth was rapid and sediments rapidly buried undecayed vegetation. Over time, these buried plants became the giant coal fields that extend from Pennsylvania west all the way into Texas.

North America was colliding into the Africa subplate. As a result of this pressure, the Appalachian Mountains were driven up to rugged heights. Approximately 290 million years ago, all the continents were joined together to form a huge "super continent" geologists call Pangaea. The Appalachians, then as high as the present-day Rockies, blocked moisture flow across the land and a desert climate dominated much of the North American continent.

Then, approximately 200 million years ago, North America began to split off from Pangaea. As it moved westward, the Atlantic Ocean was created in its wake. Thus, new continental shelves and shallow seas were formed. In addition, as the continents moved apart, plants and animals were isolated on the various continental plates, encouraging greater evolutionary divergence.

The next glimpses of Big Bend's past begin approximately 136 million years ago. At this time, shallow seas covered much of what would become the park. We know this because extensive marine fossils appear in the rocks of Big Bend, including clams and oysters. The limey shells of these animals helped to form the thick limestone deposits now exposed in the Sierra del Carmen, Mariscal Mountain, Mesa de Anguila and elsewhere. As any observant river floater has no doubt noted, the rocks that make up Santa

Left: The rock wall in the middle distance of this view of the Chisos is an igneous dike, formed when magma forced itself through a crack in the rock and hardened in place.

Facing page, top: The rock in Santa Elena Canyon is mostly limestone, laid down in ancient seas.
Bottom: Goat Mountain shows the volcanic Chisos Formation, covered by the younger South Rim Formation.

Elena, Mariscal and Boquillas canyons all look similar. And so they are. In each canyon, the Rio Grande has carved through massive layers of limestone including the Glen Rose, Del Carmen and Santa Elena formations. These same sedimentary rocks underlie the intervening valleys between these canyons, but in some locations they are still buried under overlying rock layers.

Although the sedimentary block mountains of Big Bend all are composed of rocks of marine origin,

Dinosaurs once wandered this landscape; their bones are exposed in the Aguja and Javelina formations

——— ☆ ———

the rock layers vary in hardness and cohesiveness. Hence, mountain ranges like the Sierra Del Carmen tend to have a step-like, terraced conformation due to differential weathering of rocks of varying hardness. For example, in Mesa de Anguila, through which the Rio Grande has carved Santa Elena Canyon, the Del Carmen and Santa Elena limestone formations tend to form sheer cliff-faces, while the softer Sue Peaks formation erodes into sloping terraces. The first part of the hike along the Santa Elena Canyon nature trail winds along one of these terraces of softer rock.

By the latter Cretaceous period, the shallow seas were fluctuating in depth, alternately covering and uncovering the landscape in this region. Limey muds were deposited along the shore to become the shales of the Boquillas Formation and the younger Pen Formation. In places, these younger rocks still cover the older limestones. However, you won't find the younger rocks atop the highest portions of Mariscal Mountain and the Mesa de Anguila and Sierra del Carmen Mountains because erosion already has stripped them

away. One good, readily accessible location to see the layered structure of the Boquillas formation is at the mouth of Tornillo Creek by Hot Springs.

During the upper Cretaceous period, the seas were replaced by lowland swamps or bayous. Dinosaurs, at the height of their development, wandered this landscape. Their bones, along with fossilized tree stumps, are found in the Aguja and Javelina formations exposed in the lower elevations of Big Bend National Park.

The dinosaurs, as well as many other kinds of animals, suddenly disappeared approximately 65 million years ago. Many theories have been promulgated to explain these extinctions, including one that proposes a massive meteorite collision with earth. Dust from the collision may have blocked sunlight, sufficiently cooling earth's temperature to cause the massive extinctions. However, not all geologists agree with this theory, and the evidence is fragmented enough to be inconclusive.

The dinosaurs' disappearance provided new ecological opportunity for earth's surviving fauna, which included the small furry animals we call mammals. With competition from the dinosaurs gone, mammals diversified into many new forms. The Cenozoic Era began at the close of the Age of Dinosaurs and continues up to the present. It is otherwise known as the Age of Mammals. At the beginning of this era, approximately 65 million years ago, the Big Bend landscape was low and flat with swampy lakes and

Left: In Boquillas Canyon, one can see a fault where movement shifted two blocks of the earth past each other, with the rock strata of one block now higher than the matching strata in the facing block.

Facing page: Reflections in Ernst Tinaja. A series of water holes carved by a stream into the limestone layers of the Deadhorse Mountains is an important water source for wildlife.

meandering rivers. Early mammal forms were abundant and at least 29 species have been found in the sedimentary rocks of Tornillo Flat, including a small horse-like animal, a hippopotamus and an animal like a mountain lion.

Mountains and volcanoes

Approximately 175 million years ago, the North American plate began to collide with the Pacific plate. The Pacific plate was forced under the lip of the North American plate, and gradually these oceanic rocks were driven deep into earth's mantle, where they melted. The buckling and compression of the western edge of the North American plate gradually created highlands, while the shallow seas from which came many of the sedimentary rocks now found in Big Bend disappeared. Further uplift eventually gave rise to the mountains we now know as the Rockies and Mexico's Sierra Madre.

The compression caused by the collision and subduction of tectonic plates produced cracks in earth's surface, which we call faults. At times, entire blocks of rock were down-dropped along these fractures, producing the straight-lined faces that mark such Big Bend mountains as the Mesa de Anguila, seen at the mouth of Santa Elena Canyon. Another illustration of this type of down-dropping is the ruler-straight face of the dramatic Sierra del Carmen in Mexico, visible from Rio Grande Village. The Ross Maxwell Scenic Drive along the western edge of the Chisos Mountains follows a valley marked by the Burro Mesa Fault.

Volcanic activity began perhaps as early as 70 million years ago, but was at its height by 38 million years ago. Molten rock deep in the earth, probably formed from the melting of the Pacific plate, moved up through cracks in the graben and erupted as a volcano centered in the present-day Sierra Quemada. Lava flows and eruptions continued on and off for several million years, and today we see these flows and ash

47

falls preserved as the Chisos Formation. A second volcano was centered in what we know today as Pine Canyon. Lost Mine Peak and Crown Mountain mark the edge of this caldera. The volcano released magma between 33 and 31 million years ago to create the South Rim Formation. This massive flow spread over the landscape burying the earlier Chisos Formation.

Not all the magma reached the surface. Some cooled in place beneath layers of sedimentary rock, which later eroded away to expose the igneous rock beneath. The result was the dome-like formation geologists call a *laccolith*. Laccoliths in Big Bend include the Paint Gap Hills, Grapevine Hills and the Rosillos Mountains.

In the heart of the Chisos Mountains lies the Basin, a valley as deep as 2,000 feet below the surrounding high peaks. Most people mistake the basin for a volcano crater, and indeed it appears like one.

The Basin was formed when an anticline was uplifted millions of years ago. This increased the erosion of overlying rocks. More rapid erosion of the softer sedimentary layers in the center of the Basin left the surrounding rocks as a circular wall of peaks.

However, not all of the Basin's surrounding peaks were formed by the same geological process. Ward, Vernon Bailey and Pulliam peaks, which make up the west and northwest sides of the Basin, are all the hard,

Left top: The sheer cliffs of Casa Grande Peak in the Chisos Mountains were formed because a layer of hard volcanic rock capped layers of softer sedimentary rock, protecting them from weathering and erosion.
Bottom: The soft white volcanic-ash rock erodes easily into pillars and towers, as seen here in the Bofecillos Mountains of nearby Big Bend Ranch State Natural Area ("Big Bend Ranch State Park" to most Texans).

Facing page, left: South Rim of the Chisos Mountains, part of a lava flow that originated in a volcano near Pine Canyon.
Right: Volcanic boulders of basalt lie atop light-colored tuff and ash deposits near Cerro Castellan.

erosion-resistant remnants of intrusive rock formed where magma failed to reach the surface. Later erosion of the overlying rocks exposed these massive intrusions, leaving them behind as today's dome-shaped peaks.

Emory Peak, Toll Mountain and Casa Grande on

Tour the Ross Maxwell Scenic Drive to see evidence of the park's volcanic history

——— ☆ ———

the south and east sides of the Basin were formed differently. These mountains all are capped with lava flows that protect the softer underlying rocks from erosion. This produces square-faced peaks—hence names like Casa Grande, or "big house" in Spanish.

A massive lava flow forms the South Rim, where a 2,000-foot escarpment falls away providing the best vistas in the park. Jointing, or cracks in rock blocks, is visible along Toll Mountain and in Emory Peak. The cracks are due to rapid cooling and contraction of the magma once it was extruded onto the surface.

Volcanic landforms of Ross Maxwell Scenic Drive

One of the best areas of the park for seeing evidence of past volcanic activity is along the Ross Maxwell Scenic Drive. The first part of the route follows a fault-line valley. To the east are the Chisos Mountains and lying to the west is Burro Mesa. The rocks capping the mesa are identical to those 3,500 feet higher on Casa Grande. Geologists know that the Burro Mesa block dropped relative to the Chisos along the Burro Mesa Fault.

Prominent rock walls parallel the valley to the east of the road. These are dikes that emerged from the magma reservoir that once made up the Ward Mountain intrusion. Dikes are formed when magma in-

trudes into the bedrock along zones of weakness and solidifies in place. Later, these rocks, which were harder and more erosion-resistant than the surrounding rock, were left as vertical walls when the softer host rock eroded away. Similarly formed dikes also radiate from Dominguez Mountain near the Punta de la Sierra. After ascending to the Sotol overlook, the Ross Maxwell Scenic Drive drops down into a valley

Ultimately, the Ice Age beginning 3 million years ago began creation of the Rio Grande canyons
———— ☆ ————

with a short loop that goes to the Burro Mesa Pour-off. The beds of lava and ash that comprise Burro Mesa are easily observed as alternating light and dark bands seen along the Burro Mesa Pour-off Trail.

Farther along the Ross Maxwell Scenic Drive, visitors pass Goat Mountain, where erosion has exposed a cross-section of the peak. Later, this stream-eroded valley was filled by a new lava flow (South Rim Formation), that appears as the lighter colored rock seen in the stream-carved "V."

Just beyond Goat Mountain there is a short side road to the Mule Ear Peaks overlook. Mule Ear Peaks are a large dike like those seen earlier along the Burro Mesa Fault. Erosion has created the peak's two prongs.

Continuing on towards Castolon, you pass Tuff Canyon. Here Blue Creek has cut through compressed volcanic ash, which is called *tuff*. More tuff is visible along the road just below Cerro Castellan. Here, light-colored, almost white, beds of ash are covered with dark basalt boulders.

Cerro Castellan has visible light-colored layers of

Prickly pear cactus frames volcanic ash and tuff near Cerro Castellan.

ash capped by a dark layer of lava. Like Goat Mountain, Cerro Castellan preserves evidence of two major volcanic events—the older volcanic rocks comprising the Chisos Formation, and the younger cap rock composed of the more recent lava flows known as the South Rim Formation.

Just opposite Cerro Castellan is a fine example of a volcanic neck. Looking something like a petrified tree, a neck is formed when molten rock hardens in place. Later the softer layers of volcanic ash, cinders and other debris are easily eroded away, leaving behind the hard rock. The flowing nature of the original magma is preserved as "wood grain" giving the appearance of a tree trunk.

Creation of the Rio Grande canyons

The creation of the canyons of the Rio Grande is a relatively recent geological event. Some 3 million years ago earth's average temperature dropped, signaling the beginning of the Ice Age. Massive glaciers formed at both poles and began to move outward, the northern one eventually covering much of North America. At this same time, huge glaciers also formed in many higher western mountains. Although the Chisos and other nearby mountains were not shaped by glaciers, the change in climate did affect the face of the landscape. The deep canyons of the Rio Grande suggest that at one time there was greater water flow than occurs at present. And indeed, during the Ice Age, precipitation was higher than today.

According to a still-controversial theory, it was not the Rio Grande but the Rio Conchos that is largely responsible for the canyon formation. The channel where the Rio Grande now flows was occupied until recently by a minor tributary of the Rio Conchos. The ancestral Rio Grande flowed into a playa basin in Mexico southwest of present-day El Paso. Only in recent geological history—about 60,000 years ago—did the Rio Conchos tributary capture the

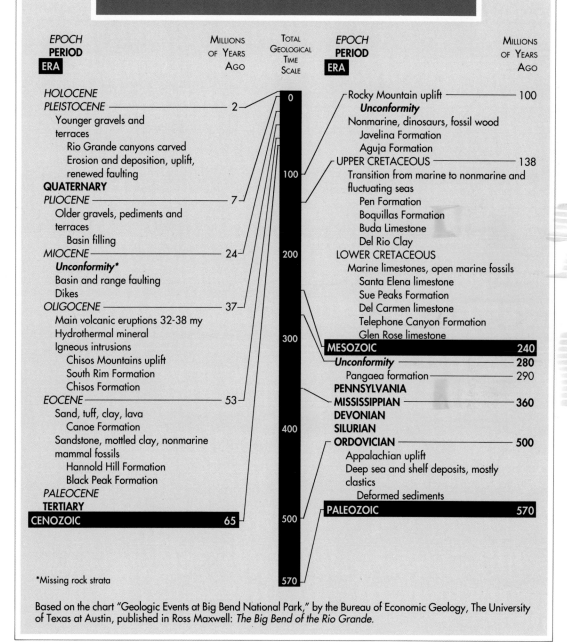

GEOLOGIC EVENTS AT BIG BEND NATIONAL PARK

EPOCH / PERIOD / ERA	MILLIONS OF YEARS AGO	TOTAL GEOLOGICAL TIME SCALE	EPOCH / PERIOD / ERA	MILLIONS OF YEARS AGO
HOLOCENE		0	Rocky Mountain uplift	100
PLEISTOCENE	2		*Unconformity*	
Younger gravels and terraces			Nonmarine, dinosaurs, fossil wood	
Rio Grande canyons carved			Javelina Formation	
Erosion and deposition, uplift, renewed faulting			Aguja Formation	
QUATERNARY			UPPER CRETACEOUS	138
PLIOCENE	7		Transition from marine to nonmarine and fluctuating seas	
Older gravels, pediments and terraces			Pen Formation	
Basin filling			Boquillas Formation	
MIOCENE	24	200	Buda Limestone	
Unconformity*			Del Rio Clay	
Basin and range faulting			LOWER CRETACEOUS	
Dikes			Marine limestones, open marine fossils	
OLIGOCENE	37		Santa Elena limestone	
Main volcanic eruptions 32-38 my			Sue Peaks Formation	
Hydrothermal mineral			Del Carmen limestone	
Igneous intrusions		300	Telephone Canyon Formation	
Chisos Mountains uplift			Glen Rose limestone	
South Rim Formation			**MESOZOIC**	**240**
Chisos Formation			*Unconformity*	**280**
EOCENE	53		Pangaea formation	**290**
Sand, tuff, clay, lava			PENNSYLVANIA	
Canoe Formation		400	MISSISSIPPIAN	**360**
Sandstone, mottled clay, nonmarine mammal fossils			DEVONIAN	
			SILURIAN	
Hannold Hill Formation			ORDOVICIAN	**500**
Black Peak Formation			Appalachian uplift	
PALEOCENE			Deep sea and shelf deposits, mostly clastics	
TERTIARY			Deformed sediments	
CENOZOIC	**65**	500	**PALEOZOIC**	**570**
		570		

*Missing rock strata

Based on the chart "Geologic Events at Big Bend National Park," by the Bureau of Economic Geology, The University of Texas at Austin, published in Ross Maxwell: *The Big Bend of the Rio Grande*.

main branch of the Rio Grande in what is now New Mexico, redirecting its flow to the Gulf of Mexico.

Prior to this geological event, the ancestral Rio Conchos had eroded away many layers of rock and already had begun to cut down into the harder, fautled rocks that now make up the canyons. The Rio Conchos, already entrenched in the canyons it had initiated, now grew greatly in volume with the added flow of the Rio Grande. But the much enlarged river, despite its greater power, could flow nowhere but in the already existing channels. The greater force of the combined rivers did mean, however, the process of canyon cutting accelerated. In time, the magnificent canyons of the Rio Grande would be the result.

Desert landforms

Although water is, by definition, scarce in a desert environment, it is nevertheless the major agent of erosion. Summer thundershowers are common in Big Bend, but the torrential showers usually run off quickly and soil absorption is minimal. In the desert, even a little water can do a lot of erosive work.

Desert stream channels tend to be wide and barren of vegetation. Most of the time they are dry as well. Local residents call them washes or arroyos. However, during a summer thundershower, these same dry channels can be transformed into seething, roiling masses of muddy water and debris, all heading pall-mall for the Rio Grande. The scouring by these periodic flash floods keeps the channels free of debris and live vegetation. A place to see one of these washes is Tornillo Creek where the bridge crosses it four miles from Rio Grande Village.

Another common desert feature is the alluvial fan. Rain falling on the barren hills and peaks gathers in ever-swelling rills and streamlets, which are funnelled down narrow canyons. With tremendous power, these flash floods can move large boulders and carry huge sediment loads down the mountain slopes. Once beyond the skirt of the mountains, and on gentler terrain, the water slows and spreads out, and the silt, sand and rocks gradually settle out. Over time, the channel braids back and forth across the mouth of the canyon, forming a fan-shaped deposit we call the alluvial fan. If several fans join together, it is referred to as a *bajada*. Such fan-shaped aprons are common along the base of the Chisos Mountains. Particularly good ones can be seen near Dominguez Mountain and the Elephant Tusk.

Besides water, wind is also a major agent of change in desert landforms. If you hike in any of the park's creosote flats, you're likely to see the wind-created desert pavement. Desert pavement forms where high winds, along with water, scour away all the small fragments of dirt, leaving behind only the heavier pebbles and cobbles. It looks almost as if these small stones were compressed together to form a road, hence its name.

Because there is little screening vegetation in Big Bend National Park, its geological history is readily observed by any visitor. Although the region's geological history still is being pieced together, and future research will no doubt change parts of the present interpretation, the region's timeless beauty—in a large part due to its geological history—will continue to be a source of inspiration and wonder.

Top: *Burro Mesa was created by a succession of volcanic eruptions and lava flows; its top layer is a hard cap of volcanic rock that resists erosion and protects the softer ash layers (visible beneath).*
Bottom left: *Lichen-encrusted volcanic rock at the head of Pine Canyon.*
Right: *Desert pavement visible along the River Road.*

Facing page: *Fluted limestone walls along Mariscal Canyon of the Rio Grande.*

53

PLANTS FROM RIVERSIDE TO MOUNTAINTOP

Above: Strawberry cactus. Many cacti respire (exchange gasses) at night when water losses are lower.

Facing page: The desert shrub zone is the lowest, hottest, driest and largest zone in the park, covering roughly half the park's acreage. Seen here are lechuguilla on limestone, with the Chisos Mountains beyond.

The ecological setting of any landscape reflects the interaction of the region's plants and animals with the physical factors such as climate, topography and geology. Big Bend's flora and fauna are strongly influenced by the area's location on the lower edge of one of North America's great aridlands—the Chihuahuan Desert. To understand why these plants and animals are here and how they cope with the desert environment, it is helpful to know why a desert exists in West Texas to begin with.

Climatic influences

Western historian Walter Prescott Webb once wrote: "At the heart of the desert there is no drought, there is only an occasional mitigation of dryness." Certainly this is true for Big Bend. Despite occasional cloudbursts, even floods, aridity is the dominant characteristic of this landscape.

The reason for this overall dryness is related to two factors—topography and world atmospheric circulation. If you look at the location of the world's major deserts on a map, a pattern becomes obvious. Nearly all deserts are located in a band between the latitudes of 15 and 30 degrees on each side of the equator. This is more than coincidence. The ultimate cause of this arid band is the pattern of global atmospheric circulation. At the equator, water evaporates into the air. Continued heating of the resulting air masses causes them to rise into the upper atmosphere. There the moist air masses are cooled and, as a result, their ability to hold moisture is decreased. Precipitation falls mostly as the heavy rain common in the tropics. The subsequently drier air masses flow away from the equator to create high-pressure systems over the Tropics of Cancer and Capricorn in the subtropics—roughly the 15 to 30 degrees north and south of the equator where the world's major deserts are found. These high-pressure air masses descend, and in the process heat up and regain their ability to hold moisture. However, since most of the moisture they once held was wrung out over the tropics, these descending air masses now behave like sponges, soaking up moisture. The air over land masses located along these latitudes is further dried. The result of this global circulation pattern is what most of us call good weather—clear skies and lots of sunshine.

The dominance of descending high-pressure over the region is only one reason for the aridity of the Chihuahuan Desert. It also owes its dryness to the rain-shadow effect of mountains. The high peaks and ridges of both the Sierra Madre Occidental and Sierra Madre Oriental, which run roughly north-south along the backbone of Mexico, present a major topographic barrier to the passage of moisture-laden air from the Pacific Ocean. By the time air masses ascend these mountain heights and cool, much of their potential moisture has been precipitated out.

Because of the above two factors, the air over much of the Southwest is capable of absorbing a great deal of moisture before it becomes saturated. In Big Bend this means that for each inch of precipitation that actually falls to the ground, as much as seven to eight *feet* could potentially evaporate into the air before it would be saturated.

The air's great ability to absorb moisture is one reason why you can take a shower at Rio Grande Village and within minutes your hair will be completely dry, as if you had just used a blow dryer on it. In a similar manner, sweat evaporates readily and keeps people cooler than they would feel at similar temperatures in more humid regions. However, because moisture is wicked away readily from the skin, a person visiting Big Bend has to drink far more water to keep from dehydrating than he or she would have to consume in, say, humid Georgia. The same problem of evaporation and dry air affects all animals and plants, except that for most living things in the desert, moisture lost due to evaporation is not easily replaced.

The lack of humidity in deserts poses another potential problem for desert dwellers. Unlike regions of high humidity where atmospheric moisture acts like a blanket to trap daytime heat, keeping it from radiating back into the upper atmosphere, at Big Bend the clear, dry desert air allows the land's surface to cool rapidly once the sun sets. It's not unusual for the daytime high to be 90° and nighttime low to be 50° or less. Large diurnal temperature extremes are the norm.

Besides the large daily temperature extremes, Big Bend country experiences seasonal extremes as well. Rio Grande Village has recorded a summer temperature of 119°, while at the opposite end of the spectrum, the thermometer there once registered 8° above zero on a crisp clear winter day—a temperature range of 111°. This is a decidedly severe environment for any plants or animals to tolerate.

Animals and plants living in the Chihuahuan Desert

also must adapt to a seasonally-variable rainfall pattern. Nearly 80 percent of the annual precipitation in Big Bend comes as a result of monsoonal thunderstorms. During summer, moisture-laden air masses from the Gulf of Mexico sweep over Big Bend, dropping their heavy water loads during violent thunderstorms. Sometimes an inch or more will fall in a single storm. The result is often what desert dwellers call a flash flood. The sudden release of water is far more than can be readily absorbed by the land and, down gullies and washes, a growing tide of water frequently changes dry land into a muddy torrent in a matter of minutes.

Winter storms, although less frequent, tend to be gentler. Rain falls over a wide area at a steady rate that can be absorbed more readily into the often hard-packed desert soils.

Finally there are year-to-year variations, as regional weather data shows. During drought years Presidio on the Rio Grande has received as little as 2.7 inches of precipitation, Mt. Locke in the Davis Mountains, site of the University of Texas McDonald Observatory, has recorded as little as 15.16 inches. As a contrast, Presidio has received as much as 23.43 inches in a wet year, while 36 inches fell on Mt. Locke. Note that the 23 inches at Presidio in a wet year is more than fell in a dry year on Mt. Locke. During the 1947-1948 drought, which occurred just after the establishment of Big Bend National Park, Johnson's Ranch on the Rio Grande inside the park received only 4.43 inches of rain. These are extreme conditions, to say the least, and yet Big Bend's vegetation must regularly endure and survive in spite of these kinds of extreme climatic variations.

Right: Honey mesquite and Cerro Castellan. Mesquite has several adaptations for desert living. Its pinnate leaves dissipate heat rapidly, while a deep root system taps water as far down as 175 feet.

Facing page: Cracked mud flat along the Rio Grande. Aridity is the dominant theme for life in this land; some areas receive only five inches of rain per year.

Year-to-year climatic variation, seasonal rainfall, temperature extremes, high evaporation rates and general aridity—these are the conditions plants and animals must cope with in order to survive in the Chihuahuan Desert. Given these conditions, what is surprising is the rich diversity of species found here. For example, Big Bend, just a small part of the Chihuahuan Desert, is home to more than 1,000 plant species.

Part of this diversity can be attributed to the habitat variety found in the park, which includes everything from pine forest to riparian wetlands. No single species can be adapted to every kind of environmental gradient found in the park. An adaptation that is favorable in one instance is less desirable in another. Therefore, we find that plants as well as animals do not occur randomly, but select specific habitats based upon a host of interacting factors such as soil texture, topography, geological strata, temperature, moisture, competition with other species, predation pressure and past climatic and human-induced environmental conditions. All of these determine what will be living where. Within Big Bend, three major vegetative formations can be found, largely determined by temperature and moisture: desert shrub, grasslands and woodlands. In addition there is the extremely restricted, but very important, riparian community found along the Rio Grande and around springs.

Left: Reeds at Glenn Springs. Where water is found, plants with no desert adaptions can survive. This riparian zone—including all the Rio Grande's margins—covers less than one percent of the park.
Facing page, top: The cottonwoods at Cottonwood Campground are a non-native species.
Bottom left: Long, lacy foliage of tamarisk, which dominates many riparian zones.
Bottom right: Cottonwood leaves are broad and not designed to conserve water; hence the species flourishes in watercourses.

Riparian community

Along the Rio Grande and some of its tributaries lies a narrow riparian zone dominated by water-dependent species like honey mesquite, giant reed, common reed, screwbean, tamarisk, tree tobacco, catclaw acacia and huisache. The native cottonwood tree, nar-

No single species of plant can be adapted to every kind of environment found in the park

————— ☆ —————

row-leaf cottonwood, is exceedingly rare in the park, and most of the cottonwoods seen at Cottonwood Campground by Castolon, as well those at Rio Grande Village, are non-native Rio Grande cottonwood. The native tree, as its name implies, has long narrow, willow-like leaves, while the Rio Grande cottonwood has more rounded heart-shaped leaves.

While most of the Big Bend lowlands are extremely arid, the zone immediately adjacent to waterways offers an entirely different environment. The plants of the arid uplands usually are drought-resistant or drought-tolerant species, that is, they are adapted to living on meager amounts of water and using it efficiently. On the other hand, the plants of the riparian zone are, for the most part, water-dependent and not particularly efficient at water usage.

One of the reasons water is important is because some plants use it for evaporative cooling. Chlorophyll, the green pigment in leaves, is heat sensitive. It breaks down at high temperatures. Since the Big Bend lowlands can be very hot, heat stress can be a problem. If water is easily available, evaporation is an excellent means of cooling leaf surfaces and this is exactly what riparian species like the cottonwood rely upon for keeping their leaf temperatures within tolerable limits. In hot weather the cottonwood is a flagrant user of

59

water, one reason why it can live only where water is readily available.

Another water-loving riparian tree is the tamarisk, or salt cedar as it is sometimes called. This plant is an "exotic" or non-native species. The tree has long, lacy, silver-green foliage resembling extremely long pine needles. It now dominates many riparian areas, crowding out native species like the cottonwood. Tamarisk was introduced into the U.S. from Africa as an ornamental, and subsequently spread into the wild.

Tamarisk has invaded more than half the park's 200 or so water sources and springs, not including the Rio Grande riparian zone where tarmarisk is already well established. Since one tree can transpire up to 200 gallons of water per day, it has the capacity to significantly lower water supplies in scattered springs, which are so important as watering holes for wildlife.

Tamarisk spreads rapidly and is nearly impossible to eradicate because it can sprout from its own stump. The Park Service is attempting to control the tree's spread through limited herbicide application; however, given the already extensive range of this plant, employees will never be able to successfully eliminate the species.

Sharing the riparian zone with the tamarisk is the honey mesquite. Although mesquite is found in the shrub and grassland zones as well, it reaches its greatest size along the river flood plain. Growing in nearly pure groves called mesquite bosques, the tree survives because it has an extremely long taproot, able to reach water at depths of 50 to 100 feet. The roots of one mesquite tree excavated in a mining operation in Tucson, Arizona reached a depth of 175 feet!

Desert shrub

Desert shrub occupies the lowest, hottest and driest parts of the park and encompasses some 49 percent of total park acreage. Dominant plants in this zone include creosote bush, leather stem, Mormon-tea, tarbush, plus numerous succulents and cacti such as lechuguilla, soaptree yucca, Torrey yucca, candelilla, blind prickly pear cactus, strawberry hedgehog cactus and ocotillo.

There are three ways of dealing with life in the arid desert environment: stay near water; evolve adaptations that decrease water losses and increase efficiency of what limited water is available; or modify so water isn't a problem. In the desert, many flowers seem to have made this third choice. They complete their entire lifecycle during the season when soil moisture is relatively abundant. The percent of annuals is higher in the desert than in any other major biome. By completing their entire lifecycles in one short season, the annuals survive periods of drought as seeds in the soil. Then, when sufficient soil moisture ensures successful germination and growth, the plants grow and mature rapidly, setting seed again before the usually meager water supplies dry up.

Some desert annuals actually have chemical inhibitors on their seeds which can be washed away only by water. The inhibitor suppresses germination until sufficient soil moisture can not only strip away the inhibitor from the seed, but also flush it from the immediate area. Less moisture comes in winter, but such rains tend to be long and soaking—the kind that will wash away chemical seed coatings. Not surprisingly, the vast majority of annuals bloom here in February, March and April.

The third way plants deal with aridity is by evolving true desert adaptations. For plants living in the drier uplands, rapid evaporative cooling such as that of the cottonwood is not a viable option. Many true desert plants deal with heat stress by reducing their individual leaf surface areas. All things being equal, a small leaf will

Right: *Torrey yucca in bloom.*

Facing page: *Prickly pear cactus blossoms. The cactus flowers are coated with a waxy material to reduce water losses. In the upper corner of the photo, note the yellow flowers of a creosote bush.*

disperse heat more effectively than a large one and a narrow leaf is better than a wide one. For this reason, the leaves of most desert plants are either small, long and narrow, or highly dissected. In this way the plants maintain a relatively large amount of photosynthetic area and still reduce heat stress by dividing their leaves into many smaller parts. The pinnately dissected leaves of the honey mesquite and catclaw acacia are fine examples of this adaptation.

Small leaf size is only one adaptation of the creosote bush, the most abundant drought-resistant plant in the park. Thousands of acres of dry, desert flats are covered with almost pure stands of this three- to six-foot-tall dark green shrub that has no main stem, but rather is a collection of branches growing from its root crown.

One secret to the plant's success is its ability to change leaf size and structure to match the degree of aridity. When water is abundant, such as during the wet season, it sports mature green leaves that are the most efficient in terms of photosynthesis, but also the least drought-resistant. As conditions become drier, the creosote bush sheds these leaves, but retains a smaller set of dark green leaves with a thick waxy cuticle, or skin, that resists water losses due to evaporation. These are the leaves you're most likely to find on the plant in winter. However, if drought becomes prolonged, even these leaves are shed and the plant grows special brown-colored leaves about half the size of the other leaves, which contain very small cell spaces that can endure dehydration without experiencing cell damage. Although the creosote bush can endure a drought with such leaves, there is a cost, as each set of leaves is lost—with a corresponding reduction in leaf surface area, photosynthetic ability lessens.

A further adaptation of creosote bush is its widely-spaced growing pattern. By reducing competition for water, each plant retains enough to sustain itself. However, this pattern is not due to chance. Each creosote bush releases a chemical toxin that inhibits establishment of other creosote bushes around its perimeter.

In the harsh environment typically inhabited by creosote bush, reproduction from seeds is extremely difficult. Proper conditions for germination and survival of seedlings may occur only once every 10 to 20 years, or at even greater intervals. Thus one reason most stands of creosote bush appear to be the same size is usually that they are all the same age, having established themselves during the infrequent years when successful germination was possible.

As added insurance, the creosote bush does not rely entirely upon seed reproduction. It also has the ability to spread vegetatively, with lower branches that touch the ground taking root, eventually developing into new plants. In places, clonal circles have developed that may be thousands of years old. One clone near Yuma, Arizona is thought to be almost 11,000 years old, and some scientists believe that creosote bushes may be the oldest living things on earth.

Another easily recognizable plant of the desert shrub zone is the ocotillo. With numerous thorn-covered long stems all growing from a central root crown, the ocotillo bears beautiful red flower clusters in the spring. During much of the year, the ocotillo lacks both flowers and leaves. However, just two to three days after a good soaking rain, it sprouts hundreds of tiny lime-green leaves. These are retained until soil moisture is exhausted, then are shed. An ocotillo may sprout and drop leaves as many as eight or nine times in a single year depending upon rainfall. However, even in years of extreme drought when the ocotillo may not

Right: Red bloom of the ocotillo. The tube-shaped flowers are a favorite of hummingbirds.

Facing page: Forty-nine percent of Big Bend is considered desert shrub environment, dominated by plants like this creosote bush, which secretes a toxic chemical to prevent other plants from growing too close, reducing competition for scarce water.

produce leaves at all, it still is able to photosynthesize—albeit at a slower rate—using chlorophyll contained in its stem.

Since water loss is obviously greater during the heat of the day, the various species of cactus and other succulents have developed an alternative means of conserving water. Unlike most plants that respire (exchange gasses like oxygen and carbon dioxide) during the day when sunlight allows photosynthesis, cactus and other succulents exchange gasses at night when humidity is higher. Their water-use efficiency is thus very high.

However, many of these same plants must bloom in the daytime when pollinators are active. Because of this, they have evolved waxy, coated flowers to reduce evaporation.

Another adaptation to the uncertain desert environment that is particularly well developed in the various species of prickly pear cactus is vegetative reproduction. Nearly all prickly pear have terminal pads that are easily detached. These quickly take root if they fall to the ground, beginning new cactus plants.

In addition, most cactus species produce tasty fruits that contain large numbers of seeds. Many species of wildlife, from mule deer to ground squirrels, enjoy feasting on these fruits. They are inadvertent disseminators of new cactus plants when they expel the seeds with their feces. Research has shown that passage through animal digestive tracts also enhances seed germination.

Big Bend has more native cactus species than any other national park—more than 70 species have been recorded here. The overgrazing that occurred prior to

Left: Candelilla grows in lower elevations of the park. It has a waxy coating to protect from water loss, and once was a source of candle wax.

Facing page: *A trademark of the Chihuahuan desert, lechuguilla looks like pointed bananas. The plant often grows in colonies.*

the park's establishment, in conjunction with fire suppression, actually has contributed to a marked increase in cactus. In particular, Englemann prickly pear, the most common cactus in the park, is one of the most pervasive indicators of overgrazing. There are large stands of prickly pear found in the Basin by the bases of Pulliam and Bailey peaks, which are not to be seen in historic photos dating from 1935—the period of excessive overgrazing before the park's creation.

In addition to all these adaptations, the cactus, taking a hint from the ocotillo (no leaves at all are better in times of drought), has eliminated leaves altogether. Instead the cactus has chlorophyll in its fleshy stems, or pads. These fleshy stems also act as water storage containers, expanding and contracting as rainfall or drought dominates.

Mormon tea and candelilla offer a further variation on the same theme. Both plants grow dozens of pencil-like one- to two-foot-long green stems filled with chlorophyll. As with the various cactus species, photosynthesis occurs in the stems themselves.

Candelilla also produces a waxy coating, in drought times, which inhibits water loss. Before the establishment of the park, candelilla was harvested and processed for its wax, which is a valuable component of records, special polishes, chewing gum and candles. The maximum amount of wax per plant was obtained from those growing on particularly dry sites.

Lechuguilla is one of the trademark plants of the Chihuahuan Desert, growing nowhere else in the world. It is particularly common on dry limestone ledges such as one finds in the Deadhorse Mountains by Rio Grande Village. However, like many plants, it grows under a wide variety of conditions and even can be found as high as the Basin in the Chisos Mountains.

Lechuguilla resembles bunches of bananas, only these are formidably spine-tipped. This is an example of another common adaptation of desert plants. Given the limited amount of living matter in the desert, almost

anything green becomes a desirable food for wildlife. To discourage browsing, many plants invest a great deal in defense. The lechuguilla is armed with sharp barbs; many cactus rely on thorns. These make it physically more difficult for animals to consume these plants. Other species rely on chemical defense. The creosote bush produces a slightly toxic substance that makes its leaves unpalatable.

Despite the threatening-looking armor of the lechuguilla, it is one of the major food items of mule deer and javelina. The latter, in particular, are very efficient at digging up the plants to get at the juicy, tender roots.

Like the creosote bush, lechuguilla reproduces by seed as well as through runners called rhizomes. This is one reason why lechuguilla tends to be found in colonies. It is also vulnerable to fire, so its widespread occurrence in the upper grassland zones—such as the Basin—is one indication of past fire suppression. It also indicates floral changes partially attributable to livestock grazing.

Grasslands

Above the desert shrub zone is the grassland zone which, like the shrub zone, also makes up 49 percent of the park. At one time the grassland component was greater, but overgrazing stripped away the grasses and exposed the soil to erosion. This reduced the soil's water-holding capacity, effectively making it more desert-like. Deep-rooted shrubs and desert-adapted plants like cactus and succulents gained a competitive edge, and they invaded many former grasslands. Meanwhile, the grassland zone migrated upslope. This zone surrounds the Chisos Mountains and is found on top of nearby mesas and mountains, usually between 3,500 and 5,500 feet.

Associated with this zone are such grasses as black grama, chino grama and side oats grama, as well as

Grasses in the Chisos Mountains.

THE GIANT DAGGER

The most unique yucca in the park is giant dagger. In the U.S. it is limited to West Texas; Big Bend National Park is one of the major centers of its distribution. Within the park, giant dagger is found primarily in the Dead Horse Mountains and is easily viewed at Dagger Flats. Most concentrations of giant dagger are found east of the Old Ore Road. However, several isolated individuals or small groups can be found in and around the Chisos Mountains, including Green Gulch, in the Basin, on the South Rim, and near the mouth of Pine Canyon. Other small groups are located near Chilicotal and Nugent mountains.

Growing up to 15 feet in height and two to three feet in width, the plant derives its name from its six-inch-wide and four-feet-long dagger-shaped leaves. Giant dagger produces a huge flowering head each spring between late March and June. The flower head grows up to five feet in length and weighs up to 80 pounds. It is covered with large white flowers. Not all flowers mature simultaneously, but instead blossoms open first near the bottom of the stalk and progress upward.

Giant dagger, like most yuccas, depends upon insect pollination. Ants are important pollinators, attracted to the flowers by their high sugar content. But the most special relationship exists between yuccas and the yucca moths. The female yucca moth has special tentacles attached to her head so she can gather pollen. The pollen is worked into a small ball and placed in a natural cavity designed for this purpose under the moth's head.

After gathering a sufficient amount of pollen the moth then forces it down into the flower pistil using a bobbing motion to jam it in securely. This ensures pollination and thus seed development. The moth backs down the pistil and punctures the ovary wall with her ovipositor and deposits her eggs—no more than six eggs per flower.

After the eggs hatch, the young moth larvae live for two weeks on sap, then, after the yucca seeds mature, the larvae bore their way into the seeds and live upon the nutritious inner core. They remain here until the seeds mature. Although the larvae destroy some seeds, far more survive, ensuring survival of the yucca upon which the moth depends.

After several more weeks of growth, the larvae bore their way out of the yucca fruit and, exuding a silk thread as an anchor, drop to the ground. The larvae then burrow into the ground and create cocoons out of soil particles and their silk thread. They stay in the ground through the winter, pupating and emerging as full adults the following spring, just days before the giant dagger flowers.

Due to the moth's pollination efforts, seed production is successful almost every year. Nevertheless, the adverse climatic conditions see to it that few seeds actually survive to the seedling stage. In order to achieve successful reproduction, regardless of environmental conditions, the giant dagger, like many desert plants, relies upon vegetative reproduction. It is not unusual to find clusters of young daggers surrounding one aging mature plant. Basal shoots produced by the older plant eventually take root, starting a new generation of daggers.

Giant dagger. Unique in the U.S. to the Big Bend area, this yucca grows to be 15 feet or more in height.

yuccas and succulents like the havard agave, giant dagger, sotol, Torrey yucca and beargrass. Shrubs include cat's claw mimosa, pink mimosa, agarito, allthorn and desert olive.

Grasses are wonderfully adapted to arid climates, particularly those with seasonal precipitation as is found in Big Bend. Most are perennial, which means they live more than one year. In fact, many individual grass plants may live for a hundred years or more. They survive in the dry Southwest by avoiding drought altogether. Most grasses grow rapidly during the rainy season, which in the Big Bend country is summer. Then when drought sets in, the aboveground leaves die and many of the nutrients contained in them are transferred to the roots where they are stored until the next growing season. At this point, most of the plants become dormant until the next rainy season. They thereby eliminate the need for additional food production.

Grasses are also well adapted to surviving frequent fires. Soil is excellent insulation and the heat from most fires will not kill grass roots. Although a fire may consume the leaves, it usually does little harm to the living roots. These immediately send up new shoots the next growing season. As a further adaptation, under all but the most severe conditions, most grasses simply will not carry a flame until the aboveground leaves are dead and dried. For these reasons, fires do no long-term damage to grasslands, and in fact may be critical for the health and persistence of these ecosystems. Fire, for example, gives grasses the competitive advantage over shrubs, cactus and yuccas, which tend to invade grasslands in the absence of fire.

But the long-practiced policy of fire suppression (this policy has been replaced by prescribed natural fires and prescribed control burns) is not the only reason grasslands have declined somewhat in vigor. The overgrazing of the Big Bend area, before the establishment of the national park, favored shrubs and cactus over grasses. Grazing eliminated much of the grass cover, with a consequent reduction in fuel. Ground cover became too sparse to carry a flame. In addition, the stress caused by heavy grazing reduced the overall growth of grass root systems, and thereby decreased each grass plant's ability to survive during drought years. Fortunately, with the removal of livestock, many of the park's grasslands are recovering from the years of abuse.

To the non-scientist, it is sometimes difficult to understand why livestock grazing should hurt grasslands, while something like wildfire can be said to be healthful. The reason is that a grassland (or any other community or living thing) is more than a collection of grass plants. It is a process: the interaction of grasses with all kinds of environmental factors, such as wildfire, insect attacks, browsing pressure, drought, flood, cold and heat.

The grasslands of Big Bend evolved under a regime of periodic fires, an ecological process which they not only tolerate, but also in fact depend upon. Just as the tremendous amount of rainfall that occurs in the tropical rainforest is not destructive to that particular plant community, fire is not the enemy of the grasslands. However, when humans introduce a new regime onto the grassland community, such as heavy livestock grazing, the community is forced to change radically, or even disappear. It has not evolved to cope with these new circumstances.

Not all parts of a grassland burn regularly, even under natural conditions. In these areas, one will often

Right top: Agave, sometimes called century plant, produces a flowering stalk when between 10 and 20 years old, which may grow to 20 feet in height. Then the plant dies.
Bottom: Decayed center of an agave makes an interesting pattern in Green Gulch.

Facing page: In the Sierra Quemada, grass quickly covered the ground after a 1981 fire. Overgrazing and fire suppression have made shrubs more common in the park than in presettlement times.

find sotol, a plant whose serrated, narrow leaves grow in clusters about three to four feet in height. The tough, serrated leaves help to discourage browsing and the narrow width increases heat dispersal. In spring, sotol produces a five- to 12-foot-long flowering stalk crowned by a spike of white flowers. The distinctive stalks often remain intact long after the flowers have died and are one means of identifying this species. A good place to see this plant is at the Sotol Overlook on the Ross Maxwell Scenic Drive.

Sotol was an important plant to the Indian cultures. The soft heart was roasted in pits and eaten, the tough leaves were used for making rope and mats, and an intoxicating drink can be made by fermenting the heart.

Woodland formation

The various mountain ranges that dot the entire trans-Pecos region are like islands in a desert sea. The higher summits are cooler and receive more moisture than surrounding lowlands, hence many species typically associated with cooler, more northerly climates can be found here. The Chisos Mountains are one such island. The highest reaches tower more than 6,000 feet above the Rio Grande lowlands, with a resulting difference in climate between upper and lower elevations.

For example, summer temperatures are 10 to 15 degrees cooler in the mountains than along the river, while winters are correspondingly colder, with 20 to 30 days of below-freezing temperatures expected during the average winter. Annual precipitation in the Basin, at 5,400 feet, is approximately 16 inches a year, six more inches than falls at Rio Grande Village. The highest mountaintops probably receive more than 20 to 25 inches a year. However, not only is there more precipitation, but due to overall cooler air temperatures, potential evaporation is lower. The net effect is a substantially moister environment.

Aspect also affects plant distribution. Even within the Basin, at better than 5,000 feet, one can find desert shrub species like the lechuguilla on the warm south-facing slopes. At the same elevation but on the north slopes, one will find coniferous forest.

These coniferous forests are part of the woodland zone that represents relict populations of what were once more widely occurring species. Examination of ancient pack rat middens preserved in caves shows that 12,500 years ago, at the end of the Ice Age, the vegetation of the Big Bend region differed substantially from today's. The climate was cooler and wetter and as

At the end of the Ice Age, Big Bend's climate was cooler and wetter, and woodland covered most of the desert shrub area

———— ☆ ————

a consequence, woodlands covered most of the lowlands now occupied by desert shrub. Piñon pine and juniper were growing along Maravillas Canyon, just east of the present park border in what is now Black Gap Wildlife Area. There are no indications that typical lowland species of today such as creosote bush and tar bush were present at that time.

Beginning around 11,500 years ago and continuing more or less unabated since then, the climate has warmed and dried. By 8,000 years ago, the vegetation typical of the Chihuahuan desert as we know it today was well established. During this same period, the woodlands migrated up the mountains seeking the cooler heights. In the lower mountains many of the woodland species disappeared altogether. In others, such as the Chisos, relicts remain.

Right: Piñon-juniper forest in Green Gulch, Chisos Mountains.

Facing page: Texas madrone has sleek, smooth bark and sometimes is called lady's legs. It grows in high, well watered canyons of the Chisos.

Trapped on the higher parts of the Chisos are Arizona cypress, Douglas fir, western yellow pine (long thought to have been ponderosa pine), Mexican piñon pine, drooping juniper, alligator juniper, red berry juniper, Texas madrone, aspen, Texas buckeye and big tooth maple.

Some of these species, such as the Western yellow pine, Douglas fir, big tooth maple and aspen are northern species approaching their southernmost limits in these mountains. All have highly restricted ranges within the Chisos Mountains.

A number of these relict species are typically associated with environments where periodic fires are commonplace. For these species, light fires eliminate competing shrub species and even thin out members of their own species. The remaining trees are healthier and better able to resist disease and insects. In forests where fire is excluded, stands become overstocked, as well as bug- and disease-infested.

Fires also assist in biological breakdown of organic matter. In the arid western environment where decomposition by bacteria and fungi is rare, fire is the major agent contributing to nutrient recycling. Dead litter decays so slowly that, without fire, this litter simply piles up on the forest floor. Eventually, these fuels build to such proportions that any fire tends to be hotter and more destructive.

Because of findings such as these, the old policy of immediate fire suppression everywhere in many parks and natural areas has been replaced with one that recognizes the natural role of wildfire in the ecological scheme of things. From an ecological perspective, it is fire suppression that kills a forest, while periodic burns actually contribute to healthy forests.

Western yellow pine is one such fire-adapted tree. It is found primarily in Pine Canyon and Boot Canyon and flourishes where there are periodic but low-intensity fires. Its thick, flaky bark protects it from all but the hottest fires. In addition, larger specimens are self-pruning, losing their lower branches so flames cannot jump easily into the tree crowns.

Another fire-adapted species is the Douglas fir. It has adaptations similar to those of the ponderosa pine, including a thick corky bark and a self-pruning habit. Douglas fir is one of the most valuable timber trees in the U.S. and, in the Pacific Northwest, this species reaches heights of 250 feet and diameters of 10 feet. However, in Big Bend, Douglas firs are restricted to the highest canyons and peaks and the largest individual is only 72 feet tall. Douglas fir are found in the Guadalupe Mountains on the Texas-New Mexico border, as well in the Chisos Mountains, but are absent from the Davis Mountains that lie between.

Aspen is another Ice Age relict that is dependent on fire. One of the most abundant trees of the southern Rockies, aspen is rather restricted in distribution in Texas. It spreads primarily by clonal root suckering, particularly after fires. Although quite common farther north, only 225 individual aspen trees are known to exist in Big Bend, all on the cooler slopes of Emory Peak. The state champion tree, a specimen four feet in diameter, is found here.

The maple found in the Chisos Mountains is an intergrade between the sugar maple of the East and the bigtooth maple of the West. Growing in a number of the higher, cooler canyons, it is one of the more beautiful trees coloring Big Bend in the autumn. Usually maples are small trees not more than 10 to 20 feet in height, but one in Pine Canyon is 60 feet tall and 4.2 feet in diameter. This giant has the title of Texas state champion.

Arizona cypress is another oddity. This beautiful, stately tree is far more common in the mountains of

Right: One of the more beautiful flowers in Big Bend is the rock nettle.

Facing page: Drooping juniper in the Chisos.

New Mexico and Arizona, but is found in Texas only in the Chisos Mountains. It is typically one of the largest trees in the Chisos Mountains, towering over other species. One specimen 112 feet tall has been found. Arizona cypress is restricted to the cooler parts of Boot Canyon and along the East Rim. It is also found across the Rio Grande in the Sierra Fronteriza of Mexico.

Growing at the lower edge of the woodland zone, typically in a savanna-like setting, is the red berry juniper. Like all the junipers in the park, it has narrow, finger-like needles with overlapping scales that help to disperse heat and reduce water losses. Of the three juniper species in Big Bend, it is the most drought-resistant, and is the juniper you'll see in the lower parts of Green Gulch as you drive up toward the Basin.

Preferring the moister conditions of the Basin and even higher elevations is the tallest of the Big Bend junipers, the alligator juniper. One tree recorded in Big Bend is eight feet in diameter and 33 feet tall. Alligator juniper gets its name for its roughly crosshatched bark, which resembles alligator skin.

The third juniper, drooping or weeping juniper, is found nowhere in the U.S. except Big Bend. As its name suggests, it is characterized by lacy, drooping branches. Its bark peels off in long, fibrous strips. The National Champion drooping juniper occurs in Juniper Canyon, has an 8.5-foot girth and is 55 feet tall.

Oaks are very difficult to identify by species. They interbreed and hybridize readily. Some 17 varieties of oaks are thought to occur in the park, but at least one authority believes these can be lumped into nine species. Some of these oaks attain tree proportions, while others are more typically shrubs. Some are evergreen and others deciduous, losing their leaves each fall. The most common oaks likely to be encountered are the gray oak, Emory oak and Grave's oak. Other oaks include the Gambel oak, which occurs on Casa Grande Peak, Chinkapin oak found in Pulliam Canyon, and lateleaf oak, an endemic found only in Boot Canyon and below El Pico in the Sierra Del Carmen. The Chisos oak, also an endemic, is restricted to Blue Creek Canyon, Juniper Canyon and the old Nail Place.

Two shrub oaks are Coahuila scrub oak, which makes up the chaparral found at Laguna Meadows in the Chisos Mountains, and Vasey oak, found primarily in the Deadhorse Mountains but also in the Chisos Mountains.

Compared to the seeds of many other plants, acorns are very large and thus, in a relative sense, an oak tree cannot produce nearly as many seeds as a tree with small seeds, such as aspen or cottonwood. However, the oak's strategy is to invest a lot of energy into each seed, and thus a better chance of success—that is, germination and eventual growth into a mature tree. By making its seed edible, the oaks ensure that animals like the squirrel and acorn woodpecker will carry some of its seeds away from the parent tree. Animals such as the squirrel may even bury it, ensuring a good chance of germination.

Following the same strategy as the oaks is the Mexican piñon pine—one of the more common species found in Big Bend. Each cone contains several dozen very large nutritious seeds, or pine nuts as they are called. Gray breasted jays, common in the Chisos Mountains, often pick open the cones to get at the tasty nut inside. Many other animals—including black bear, gray fox and many rodents—also eat piñon nuts whenever they can find them.

Piñon pine is common along Green Gulch, in the Basin, on the South Rim and elsewhere in the park. It is more drought-resistant than yellow pine so tends to be found at lower elevations or in drier habitats.

Right: Fern in Green Gulch. Although Big Bend is very arid, it has moist pockets where a veriety of ferns can be found.

Facing page: Oak covered with lichens. The park supports nine species of oak, plus numerous hybrids.

CHRISTIAN HEEB

Above: Vermilion flycatcher.

Facing page: The bobcat is found throughout the park and hunts mostly smaller rodents and rabbits. It differs from the mountain lion, also found in Big Bend, by being much smaller and having a bobbed tail instead of the lion's long one.

WILDLIFE IN DIVERSE HABITATS

Since all wildlife is ultimately dependent on suitable habitat, the great variety of plants at Big Bend—from riverside vegetation to mountain pine forest—obviously presents many different habitat opportunities for wildlife. The result is a profusion of wildlife in Big Bend.

Birds

One of the most surprising facts about Big Bend's wildlife is that the park has recorded more species (434) of birds than any other unit in the national park system—more than the Everglades, more than Great Smokies, more than the Olympic Mountains and a host of other areas which would seem, initially, to present more suitable avian habitat. Yet, during the course of a year in Big Bend, it is possible to see nearly half the total number of bird species recorded for the entire United States and Canada! However, fewer than 10 percent are year-round residents.

Four major classes of birds use Big Bend: migrants, winter residents, summer breeders, and those summer visitors that come to Big Bend after breeding elsewhere. As might be suspected, migrants make up the largest category, especially since the Rio Grande is a major flight pathway for birds moving north or south.

During migrations it's possible to see many species one would not ordinarily associate with Big Bend. For example, during a canoe trip on the Rio Grande one example, during a canoe trip on the Rio Grande one April, I saw a lone snow goose resting on a sand bar. The snow goose normally nests on the tundra in the far north, but winters in Mexico and along the Texas Gulf Coast.

For more specific information about birding in Big Bend National Park, former Chief Naturalist Roland Wauer's book, *A Field Guide to Birds of the Big Bend*, is highly recommended.

The best time for seeing birds in migration is from mid-March through late April. During this period, ducks and other waterfowl, shorebirds, hawks, sparrows and warblers all move through in large numbers. There are, for example, 52 species of warblers recorded for Big Bend, nearly all of which are migrants. Only five are known to nest in the park.

Winter resident birds are the next-largest group. Since Big Bend is so far south, many northern birds spend their winters here, just as many humans do. Depending on the severity of the winter, species likely to be seen include nesting robins, hermit thrush and dark-eyed junco.

More than a hundred species are breeders—birds that actually produce young in the park. Although many are associated with specific habitats within the park, because birds are more mobile than plants, generalizing about species locations is somewhat hazardous. For example, white-winged doves can be found nesting in the riparian zone along the river as well as in

the open woodlands of the Chisos Mountains. Yet the Colima warbler is fairly restricted to the moist oak woodlands in the higher reaches of the Chisos Mountains.

A rich collection of nesting birds favors the floodplain-riparian zone, even though it accounts for the smallest acreage of plant community in the park. In fact, it has far and away the largest number of nesting birds per acre. Count on seeing nesting mourning doves, the white-winged dove, pyrrhuloxia, Bell's vireo, northern mockingbird, yellow-breasted chat, hooded oriole, painted bunting, northern cardinal, brown-headed cowbird, black-tailed gnatcatcher, yellow-billed cuckoo, roadrunner, ladder-backed woodpecker, black phoebe, verdin, black-chinned hummingbird and the difficult-to-see screech owl.

In the thicker stands of mesquite, cactus and other vegetation found along desert washes, one will likely encounter the cactus wren, northern mockingbird, pyrrhuloxia, scaled quail and lesser nighthawk.

Desert shrub is the largest plant community in the park; however, its overall diversity is limited. Not surprisingly, far fewer species of birds are found here than in any other area of the park. Except for extremely small birds that can nest in the small shrubs and cactus characterizing this zone, most nesters utilize the ground or cliffs. The open country is excellent terrain for raptors. Many of the park's birds of prey are found here, including common ravens, kestrels, great horned owls, golden eagles, turkey and (rarely-seen) black vultures, zone-tailed and red-tailed hawks. In addition, small passerine species like rock wrens, canyon wrens, black-throated sparrows and white-throated swifts typically are associated with the desert shrub zone.

Just beyond the desert shrub zone is the grassland zone, second largest of the park's major habitat types. Nesting here are cactus wrens, black-tailed gnatcatchers, northern mockingbirds, black-throated sparrows, pyrrhuloxias, verdins, ash-throated flycatchers, common poorwills, roadrunners, elf owls, Scott's orioles, black-chinned sparrows, rufous-crowned sparrows, blue grosbeaks, varied buntings and brown towhees.

Finally we come to the second smallest habitat in the park after the riparian—the woodland zone. This includes the open piñon pine-juniper-oak woodlands located immediately above the grasslands, as well as the moister pine-oak woodlands found in the upper ends of Pine, Boot and other canyons in the Chisos Mountains.

Breeding birds likely to be encountered in the woodlands of Big Bend include the Colima warbler, bandtailed pigeon, northern flicker, western flycatcher, acorn woodpecker, gray-breasted jay, blue-throated and broad-tailed hummingbirds, rufous-sided towhee, sharp-shinned hawk, flammulated owl, Bewick's wren, zone-tailed hawk, white-breasted nuthatch, rufous-crowned sparrow and black-headed grosbeak.

Because of their rarity in the United States, among the more interesting Big Bend birds are the Mexican species that just barely pass north of the border. These attract dedicated birders who come to Big Bend, hoping to add the birds to their life lists. Some of these species can be seen nowhere else in America. Two are the dull-colored Colima warbler and the strikingly colored, green-backed, purple-throated, Lucifer's hummingbird. Both are summer breeders in the park.

Although the Colima warbler is found in the U.S. only in Big Bend, it is a fairly common summer resident in Boot Canyon, among the oaks. It appears to prefer moister habitats, but in drier years, it can be found in more open locations like Laguna Meadows. The most reliable place to see this bird is near Boot Spring.

Found in the United States only in Big Bend and southeast Arizona, Lucifer's hummingbird is rather common within this restricted range. In good years, it can be seen throughout the park from the Chisos Mountains to the Rio Grande. Like all hummingbirds, Lucifer's hummingbird uses its long, curved bill to extract nectar from flowers.

The diet of both the Colima warbler and Lucifer's hummingbird is influenced by their relatively small body sizes. The small volumes of their bodies compared to the large amount of surface area available for heat loss, make it difficult for small animals like warblers and hummingbirds to maintain proper body temperatures. As a result, such birds must eat high-energy diets that return maximum calories per unit of food. This is why a tiny bird like the Lucifer's hummingbird eats nectar—it is nearly pure sugar and thus very high octane fuel. The warbler eats insects, another food high in calories. A large bird like the Canada goose, with a small surface relative to volume, can survive grazing on grass, a food very low in energy per unit of weight.

Hummingbirds, with their overall high metabolism rate, must take things a step further to conserve on energy waste. At night they drop into a state of torpor, which economizes on heat lost by radiating into the environment.

The nectar-eating habit of the hummingbird is not only beneficial to the bird, but is important also for the pollination of flowers. Some plants even have flowers specifically designed to accommodate hummingbirds and other bird species. Such flowers tend to be shaped into long, narrow tubes, like those of the tree tobacco plant and the ocotillo.

Although the Lucifer's hummingbird and Colima warbler are rare in the United States, they are fairly common within their normal range, which extends into Mexico. However, there are within Big Bend species rare in the park as well as throughout their entire breeding range. One such bird is the black-capped vireo, whose range includes only a small portion of

ABOVE: FREDERICK D. ATWOOD; BELOW: CHRISTIAN HEEB

Right top: Roadrunners are common at lower elevations where they hunt snakes, lizards and other reptiles.
Bottom: Pyrrhuloxia.

Facing page: Golden eagles occasionally nest in the park and also are seen as migrants. For years, ranchers shot these birds even though protected, but now their numbers appear to be stable.

Texas and Oklahoma. It is now listed as an endangered species by the U.S. Fish and Wildlife Service. This bird typically is found in oak thickets in canyons of the Chisos Mountains. In 1985 only six singing males were seen in the park. Sightings in 1986 documented only four singing males, but this subsequently increased to nine in 1987. Nevertheless, the black-capped vireo is in a precarious position.

The vireo's troubles stem from brood parasitism by the brown-headed cowbird, whose numbers have increased in the area. The cowbird slips into the vireo's nest and lays one of its own eggs. Unfortunately birds cannot count and the vireo never notices the added egg, even though it is quite a bit larger than its own. Instead it broods the cowbird's egg along with its own. The cowbird chick usually hatches a day or two earlier than its host species' own young. The vireo, thinking the giant youngster is one of its own, begins feeding it. After the vireo eggs hatch, the much larger juvenile cowbird often crowds the other birds from the nest or at the least, because of its greater size and aggressiveness, gets the lion's share of food.

Black-capped vireos are not the only Big Bend birds parasitized by cowbirds. Other species include blue grosbeak, painted bunting, black-throated sparrow, Bell's vireo, black-tailed gnatcatcher, yellow-breasted chat, and the house sparrow. Brood parasitism by cowbirds is suspected to be the main reason behind the local extinction of the yellow warbler, which used to be a fairly common nester along the Rio Grande.

Adult cowbirds are attracted to areas with livestock, which accounts for their name. In an example of "unnatural" history, the horse corrals within the Basin and near Panther Junction are one of the main attractions for this livestock-loving bird. To reduce cowbird populations, the NPS has removed them both into the Basin and Panther Junction, with 200 birds removed in 1986 and 400 more in 1987.

Another Big Bend endangered species is the sleek

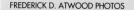

peregrine falcon. Known to dive at speeds of up to 200 miles per hour, this raptor feeds primarily on other birds. Big Bend falcons prey mostly on the mourning dove, white-winged dove and gray-breasted jay.

The peregrine, never abundant, suffered major population losses after World War II with the widespread application of pesticides like DDT. These pesticides were ingested by prey species as they ate insects or crops dusted with the chemical. The chemicals were further concentrated in the falcon when it ate the DDT-contaminated birds. As result of high pesticide levels within their bodies, peregrines produced thinner egg shells and consequently suffered more nest failures.

Although DDT was banned in the United States, it is still legal for American companies to produce and export the chemical. Hence, as use in the U.S. declined, companies expanded its use in other countries, including Mexico. The Carter Administration sought to ban or at least regulate exports, but the Reagan Administration reversed this and and in fact loosened regulation of pesticides by the Environmental Protection Agency. Ironically, DDT is smuggled back into the U.S. from Mexico and illegally applied to crops in Arizona, New Mexico and Texas, including some within the Rio Grande drainage.

Despite the impacts of pesticides on peregrines in general, Big Bend and the surrounding Chihuahuan Desert have had one of the most stable peregrine populations in the country, due in part to the remoteness and lack of agriculture. Also, nearly all the breeding peregrines in the region are non-migratory—they do not travel to other places where they may be contaminated. However, even the local peregrines exhibit evidence of pesticide poisoning, partially because many prey species they eat are migratory and bring the toxic chemicals from elsewhere.

In 1987 there were nine documented peregrine eyries (nests) within Big Bend. In 1988 researchers recorded the successful fledging of seven young.

Peregrines nest only on cliffs. These provide protection from most mammal predators. However, suitable habitat is not that easily obtained. For one thing, peregrines in the Big Bend region nest only on large cliff faces which are hundreds of feet tall. One peregrine study conducted by the Chihuahuan Desert Research Institute in nearby portions of Mexico discovered an example of niche separation between the peregrine falcon and the similar prairie falcon. No active peregrine nest was found on cliffs less than 300 feet high, while no prairie falcon cliff was above 250 feet, and most were less than 100.

Even when the falcons are nesting hundreds of feet above the ground, they still are very sensitive to intruders. The mere presence of humans is enough to disturb them. Excited birds will shriek repeatedly with high piercing calls. One of the ways researchers locate nest sites is by passing through suspected peregrine habitat and waiting for such a response.

Nevertheless, if visitors hear the worried calls, they should leave the area immediately. Peregrines have been known to abandon desirable nest sites for less suitable ones, and even have abandoned growing young if disturbed too frequently. Just a short absence from the nest site leaves the peregrine's offspring vulnerable to predation from other birds of prey. Great horned owls, for example, are notorious predators on young peregrines. This is one reason why the Park Service has taken to closing certain park trails during peregrine nesting season, and it is important for peregrine survival that such closures be observed.

One of the more conspicuous birds likely to be seen

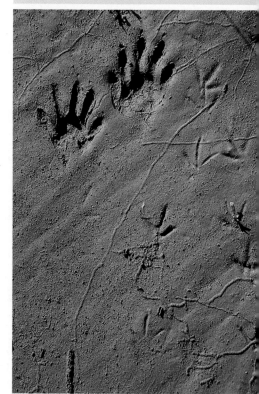

Right top: Tracks of a raccoon, spotted sandpiper and earthworm.
Bottom: Turkey vultures often are seen soaring on thermals. They use an acute sense of smell to locate carrion.

Facing page: One of the most common avian predators in the park, the great horned owl has such acute hearing that it can locate prey in total darkness.

in the Chisos Mountains, particularly around the Basin, is the acorn woodpecker. This black and white bird with a red cap is a comical sight, dressed up like a clown. Its raucous call is a distinctive feature of the oak woodlands, which produce the bird's favorite food—acorns.

The woodpeckers collect acorns, particularly in the fall, and cache them in holes they have drilled in old snags, fence posts or other suitable sites. As many as 50,000 acorns have been found stored in one tree. Later, in winter, the birds revisit these granaries and extract the nuts as needed.

Acorn woodpeckers live in small colonial flocks of genetically-related brothers, sisters and cousins. Colonial living probably benefits the woodpecker in several ways. First, with several pairs of eyes on the lookout, predators are more easily spotted and avoided. In addition, by working cooperatively when a good acorn source is located, all birds can share in the bounty, increasing the survival of the family units.

The gray-breasted jay is another common resident of the Chisos Mountains. Like the acorn woodpecker, it lives in large flocks and probably derives many of the same benefits from communal living. Gray-breasted jays are somewhat tame, and very common around the Basin campground.

Another bird seen in large groups is the scaled quail. It is found throughout the drier parts of the park below 5,000 feet. The ground-nesting quail displays several adaptations to its habitat. As might be expected, nesting on the ground offers limited protection from predators such as coyotes and bobcats. As compensation, the quail typically lays a large clutch of eggs. As many as 16 young have been counted with one Big Bend female, while it would be unusual for a cavity-nesting woodpecker, for example, to produce more than four or five eggs.

A further adaptation to the vulnerability of the quail young to predation is their precociousness. A one-day-old quail chick is fully feathered in down, alert, has its eyes open and is able to run, while a nesting sparrow of the same age is naked, blind and completely helpless. A day-old quail chick can follow its parent and begin feeding itself immediately. Obviously, this is a great boon to the mother quail, since feeding 16 young would be nearly impossible!

The lesser nighthawk is also a ground-nesting bird but, unlike the quail, it usually produces only two eggs. Its young are not precocious and the adult nighthawk has to feed and care for them while they develop. Since it hunts insects primarily at dusk and early morning, the nighthawk is somewhat restricted in its ability to feed its young. Hence, the small clutch size. Nevertheless, the longer period of parental care allows young nighthawks to develop greater coordination, flight ability and brain power than quails, and their survival rate is higher.

Mammals

Big Bend is home to 78 species of mammals. Although mammals are as interesting to most people as birds, their nocturnal habits make them more difficult to observe.

Among the most maligned but most interesting groups of mammals are bats. They comprise the largest mammal group in Big Bend, making up approximately one quarter of all species found in the park. This is not really surprising considering bats are the second-largest order of mammals, after rodents, in the world. Bats have evolved both flight and echolocation, which allow them to occupy many of the niches filled during the day by insect-eating birds. Indeed the swooping, erratic flight of the bat is reminiscent of insect-eating bird species such as swallows, swifts and nighthawks.

Bats have several general adaptations that account for their overall success. First, many bats hibernate for part of the year, thereby avoiding periods when food is not readily available. Bats also lower their metabolic needs by dropping their body temperatures into a near-torpor condition during the day, while roosting. In many caves they shift their position throughout the day to take advantage of temperature gradients. For example, by moving deep in a cave or crevice where it is cooler, the bat can quickly lower its body temperature and thereby reduce its energy needs. Then, towards evening, just before it emerges to begin feeding, the bat will move towards the mouth of the opening where temperatures are higher, passively bringing its body temperature back up to optimal flight-hunting temperatures.

Although many bats are dependent upon riparian areas and standing water for meeting their daily moisture needs, most bats are efficient users of water because they possess the ability to concentrate wastes so that water losses through excretion are dramatically reduced. This is, of course, an important feature in the desert of Big Bend. In addition, they spend most of their daylight hours in caves, which tend to have a higher humidity than the outside. Water losses are thus reduced further.

In nearly all bat species, insects account for the major portion of the diet. These are located and captured on the wing. However, if the insect is particularly large, the bat may fly to a tree or cave to consume its meal. One Big Bend bat species, the pallid bat, not only captures insects on the wing, but also has the un–bat-like habit of crawling on the ground to capture bugs like crickets, scorpions and other large prey.

While most bats eat insects, some species rely upon flower nectar and pollen, and in fact can be important pollinators of plants. Plants that are bat-pollinated tend

Right: Two kinds of large falcons are likely to be seen within the park, the peregrine and the slightly larger prairie falcon pictured here.

Facing page, top: The cactus wren is common here, building its nest in the protective spines of cholla cactus.
Bottom: The white-winged dove's cooing is a common early-morning sound around Rio Grande Village.

to flower at night. In addition, studies have shown that bats cannot survive merely on the nectar, but require protein as well, which they obtain by eating pollen. Bat-pollinated plants have evolved a form of pollen high in amino acids to supplement the nectar and thereby provide a balanced diet. This is merely another example of co-evolution, where the bat benefits from the food provided by the plant, while the plant is assured of pollination.

At least 19 species of bat have been recorded for Big Bend, including the long-nosed bat found nowhere else in the United States. The long-nosed bat, resident in the Chisos Mountains in summer and in Mexico in winter, has been listed as an endangered species by the U.S. Fish and Wildlife Service. In 1972 its population was estimated to be 10,000 individuals; a recent survey in 1988 suggested approximately 5,000 bats.

The experience of the long-nosed bat is not unique. In many parts of their range, bats have been declining because of pesticide poisoning. This occurs for several reasons. One is that they eat insects, and thus ingest the pesticide target species. Secondly, many bats migrate, so that even if they are living part of the year in a relatively pesticide-free environment like Big Bend, during the rest of the year they may be exposed to poisons. Thirdly, bats usually produce only one or two young a year, hence even a few years of reproductive failure can result in dramatic reductions of animals. One bat colony in Arizona that once housed 25 million animals was reduced by 99.9 percent over four years due to suspected pesticide poisoning.

The bat's offspring are usually produced in the spring of each year. One species recently recorded for Big Bend, the spotted bat, was discovered to produce very large young. A female captured in early summer 1969 in Big Bend almost immediately gave birth to a single baby that weighed one fourth the mother's weight! Considering the large size of young produced by some species, it is not surprising that adults often leave young behind in the bat colonies until they are mature.

Bat species recorded for Big Bend include the above-mentioned pallid bat, spotted bat and long-nosed bat, as well as the big-eared, big brown, ghost-faced, small-footed, western pipistrelle, California, red, western mastiff, Yuma, Brazilian free-tailed, cave, fringed, pocketed, and long-legged bats.

There are a number of rodent species in Big Bend and most are small and nocturnal. Perhaps the most likely to flash in front of your headlights at night is one of two species of kangaroo rats. In the park there are Ord's kangaroo rat and Merriam's kangaroo rat.

These small, light-colored rodents with long tails get their name because they hop on large hind legs like the kangaroo. Because their basic escape tactic with predators is to bounce erratically across the landscape, they tend to be found in more open country where this kind of locomotion is possible.

The various species of kangaroo rat have a number of adaptations to the arid environment. The first is that they are active largely at night when humidity is higher and temperatures are lower, and they thereby reduce water losses associated with breathing. In the daytime, they remain in their underground burrows where average humidity is much higher than outside. This further reduces water losses to the air.

The kangaroo rat also decreases water loss by countercurrent heat exchange in its nasal passages. As dry air is drawn in the nose, it is warmed and saturated with water. When it is exhaled and passes through the nasal passages, it is cooled, reducing its ability to hold moisture, with the end result that moisture is precipitated inside the kangaroo rat's nose rather than escaping to the atmosphere. As a result of this adaptation, the air exhaled by a kangaroo rat may be 15 degrees cooler than its body temperature.

The kangaroo rat also has an efficient kidney that removes most water from urine before it passes out of the body. When excreted, its urine has roughly one fifth the water of human urine. In its intestines, the kangaroo rat makes further water withdrawals, so that its feces are no more than dry pellets.

As a final adaptation to desert life, these seed-eating mammals can live without drinking water due to their ability to extract water from their food through oxidation. Their bodies can actually break down the carbohydrates in seeds into water.

However, not all desert mammals are as efficient as the kangaroo rat in living without water. Predators like the kit fox, coyote, badger and mountain lion often obtain sufficient water from the body fluids of their prey. The desert cottontail, common in the grasslands, and eastern cottontail, common in the mountains, both obtain water from green, succulent vegetation.

The cottontails have no particular adaptations to the desert, although they do live in burrows like the kangaroo rat. However, the blacktailed jackrabbit, which is quite common in the desert shrub zone, does not live in burrows. Rather it seeks out the shade of creosote bush, mesquite and cactus and tries to avoid the worst heat of the day. In addition, its large, vein-filled, mule-like ears act as mini-radiators, helping to reduce body heat by radiating the excess to the atmosphere.

The white-throated woodrat is not particularly water-efficient either. Yet, while it requires large quantities of water, it lives quite well in the arid shrublands. Its secret to survival lies in its diet, which is almost exclusively plants with high moisture contents, such as agave, lechuguilla and cactus. Cacti like the prickly pear produce a chemical—oxalic acid—which, if consumed

The diversity of habitats at Big Bend means an abundance of wildlife species
———— ☆ ————

Right: The large ears of the blacktail jackrabbit help disperse heat.

Facing page: A grassland resident, antelope once were common in the park. After livestock overgrazing extirpated them, a small herd was re-established during the 1940s.

in large quantities, is toxic to most mammals. However, the white-throated wood rat is able to metabolize oxalic acid and can subsist on quantities of cactus that would kill other mammals.

Most of the previously mentioned mammals are not likely to be seen by most visitors, except for those who wander about in the evening hours or after dark. However, some larger mammals are abroad in the daylight. Most visitors are likely to encounter either the javelina (sometimes called collared peccary) or the two species of deer found in Big Bend.

The javelina looks like a small pig with its long snout and well developed canine teeth. In Big Bend, they can be found everywhere from by the riverside, up into the Basin, and in other parts of the Chisos. Their numbers seem fairly stable now, but at the time of the park's establishment, they were less numerous than at present because overgrazing by livestock had eliminated many of the plants they rely upon for security and food. In addition, prior to the park's creation, hide and meat hunters took the animals year around.

Javelina are social animals, traveling in small groups of six to 10 animals. These animals have a well developed musk glands which produce a skunk-like odor, used to keep the animals together in dense vegetation, as well as to mark group territory boundaries. These territories are defended against intruders.

Group cohesion is also maintained by sound. As javelina feed, they make a continuous low grunting sound so that herd members keep in auditory touch with each other.

The social behavior of the javelina probably serves as a defense mechanism, since these animals have very poor eyesight. I have stood motionless without detection on numerous occasions less than 20 or 30 feet from feeding individuals, whose vision is good only at distances of 10 feet or less. Nevertheless, its sense of smell is acute, and if it picks up a foreign scent, it snorts and the entire group scampers off into the brush. Another benefit to group living is the javelina's habit of huddling together for warmth on cold winter nights.

Their major food items are lechuguilla and prickly pear cactus. It is nearly incomprehensible how they eat this food without damaging their mouths, yet I have watched them rip apart prickly pear oblivious to the thorns.

Usually females bear two young a year. However, survival of young is poor. One study of javelina in Big Bend found between 50 percent and 100 percent mortality in young depending in a large part on habitat quality. The more food and cover, the lower the death rate. Nevertheless, population growth is slow compared to that of other animals.

Another large animal, largely extirpated from the park, is the antelope. They never were particularly abundant within the park boundaries, and overgrazing and overhunting both took their tolls and all but eliminated local herds. A few antelope, descendents of a transplant, still roam the upper Tornillo Creek area.

When biologist Vernon Bailey surveyed wildlife along the border in 1901, he found desert bighorn sheep in the Rio Grande canyons and in the Chisos Mountains. Bailey's report is corroborated by accounts from early settlers who reported that sheep inhabited Mesa de Anguila, Marsical Mountain and Boquillas Canyon. Wild sheep also were known to exist in most most other mountain ranges in West Texas. But overhunting and overgrazing of wild sheep habitat by domestic livestock, combined with disease introduced from domestic stock, all contributed to the extinction of these animals in Texas by 1959. In the 1970s, a number of desert bighorns were reintroduced to several West Texas locations, including the Black Gap Wildlife Area to the east of Big Bend and more recently to Elephant Butte Wildlife Area to the north. Although it's possible that animals from these herds may eventually recolonize Big Bend, more than likely, if there are ever to be bighorns in the park, it will require direct reintroductions. Certainly the presence of wild sheep would add immensely to the park's value as a true biosphere representation of the Chihuahuan desert.

The other large mammals commonly seen during the early morning and evening, especially in the Basin, are deer. The two species of deer within the park can be distinguished from each other by habitat. In the more open country of desert shrub and grasslands lives the mule deer, named for its large mule-like ears.

Big Bend mule deer feed extensively on lechuguilla: one study found it comprised 23.8 percent of the deer's diet. Prickly pear cactus was the second most important food item. Since these plants are succulent, it may help the mule deer get additional water in this arid environment. Nevertheless, deer are most abundant where springs and other surface water are available.

The Carmen whitetail is the other deer found in Big Bend. It is more delicate in conformation than the blockier mule deer, and has a large white tail it waves like a flag when alarmed. While the mule deer is an animal of open terrain, the secretive whitetail prefers brushy habitat.

Of the four sub-species of whitetail deer in Texas, the Carmen whitetail is the smallest, and it may be the smallest whitetail found anywhere on the mainland of the U.S. The average live weight of adults is just 67 pounds—about the size of a medium-sized dog. There is some speculation as to the exact taxonomic status of this sub-species since there is a gradual intergrade with

Right: Desert bighorn sheep were found in Big Bend until around the turn of the century. A transplant program aims to reintroduce bighorns to their native habitat.

Facing page, top: Javelinas, or collared peccaries, live in small herds, grunting constantly and emitting a skunk-like smell to offset their poor eyeseight and keep herds together. *Bottom:* Badgers often obtain enough water for survival from the body fluids of their prey.

other subspecies in the mountains to the north and east of the park. Some biologists believe that whitetail deer in the Christmas, Rosillos and Chinati Mountains also contain populations of the Carmen whitetail.

The Carmen whitetail derives it name from the Sierra Del Carmen mountains just across the Rio Grande in Mexico. Big Bend National Park is the only place in the U.S. where this particular subspecies occurs. When the climate was wetter near the end of the Ice Age, this whitetail no doubt ranged throughout the entire Big Bend region. But once the climate changed and became more arid, whitetails were forced up into the cooler, wetter reaches of the higher mountains. Today, the Carmen whitetails of the Chisos Mountains are isolated from their nearest relatives in Mexico by miles of dry lowlands. In Big Bend, not surprisingly, these whitetails are found only above 4,500 feet in the brushier and forested parts of the Chisos Mountains. An occasional whitetail also may be seen in the higher parts of the Deadhorse Mountains.

Free-standing water appears to be one of the most important habitat requirements, and the whitetail is not found anywhere without perennial springs or creeks. However, deer never linger long at waterholes, since predators often wait in ambush.

The major predator of whitetails in Big Bend is the mountain lion. One Big Bend study looked at the known mortality of mule deer and whitetails and found that lions were responsible for 34 percent of the deaths, while vehicles were just behind—accounting for 30 percent of the known mortalities.

Big Bend National Park is one of the few sanctuaries for Texas' premier predator, the mountain lion. The lion is strictly a meat-eater and its primary prey is deer. However, research suggests that in parts of Mexico where deer numbers are severely depressed due to unrestricted year-round hunting, giving lions little choice, they tend to eat domestic livestock—much to the ire of ranchers. Nevertheless, where deer are readily available, lions clearly prefer venison to beef. And deer is preferred even over other wild meats, since lions seldom eat small rodents or rabbits, although they are fond of porcupines when they can get them.

Unlike a wolf that prefers to run down prey, the lion kills by ambush. Lions tend to hunt along major game trails or near waterholes. The mountain lion usually captures prey by a single bound or surprise attack, and for this reason, broken terrain or dense vegetation is important to screen its movements.

The frequency with which lions kill deer varies with the weather. In warm weather, any meat not immediately consumed rots rapidly. As a result, a lion is forced to obtain a new animal every few days. However, in cooler weather, the lion will sometimes cover the uneaten portion of a kill and return several times to finish off the remaining meat on the carcass.

So secretive is the lion that no one really knows how many are in the park. Estimates suggest that there might be 10 to 20. Most of those animals are concentrated in the Chisos Mountains where the highest deer density is found. Since human use of the Chisos Mountains is also very high, lions and humans are often in proximity. Research in Big Bend has shown that lions use the same trails as people. If bedded down, they tend to remain motionless rather than run, hence humans frequently pass relatively close to park lions and usually are completely unaware of the predator's presence.

Mountain lions will on occasion attack people. Of the number of verified lion attacks throughout North America, three occurred within Big Bend National Park. Research to date suggests that most lion attacks involve either young, inexperienced lions or adults in poor condition. In either case, the animals appear to be experiencing difficulty obtaining their usual prey and hunger appears to have motivated the attacks on humans. Nevertheless, considering the huge number of people who hike in Big Bend and other areas inhabited by lions, the chance of lion attacks is very small. Statistically,

driving the park highways is a far more dangerous activity.

Lions are protected within Big Bend now, but prior to the park's establishment mountain lions were killed at every opportunity. Homer Wilson, who ranched in the Chisos Mountains on Blue Creek, claimed to have killed 55 lions between February 1929 and December 1937. Even today, outside of Big Bend National Park, the mountain lion is subject to constant persecution. Texas, in an archaic holdover from its frontier past, is now the only state that still considers the mountain lion a predator, and does not regulate their killing whatsoever. And taxpayer dollars support the federal Animal Damage Control agency that traps, hunts and otherwise seeks to eradicate lions. Even in the Black Gap Wildlife Area immediately adjacent to Big Bend National Park, which is managed by the Texas Parks and Wildlife Department, the unenlightened policy of year-round mountain lion control prevails. In the past few years, more than 26 lions have been killed in this one area alone.

Although unrestricted hunting has not eradicated the lion, it has affected another Texas species—the black bear. Extirpated in the park by the 1940s, the only viable bear populations in Texas are found in Guadelupe National Park to the north and perhaps along the Louisiana border. Nevertheless, in recent years there have been a number of black bear sightings within the park, including several in the Chisos Mountains as well as Persimmon Gap, and along the Rio Grande River. It is speculated that bears from Mexico's Sierra Del Carmen cross the river into Big Bend National Park. And, in July

Right top: The mule deer is an animal of open shrub- or grasslands, common here wherever there is a steady supply of water in lower elevations.
Bottom: Coyotes eat mostly rabbits, rodents and birds.

Facing page: The largest predator currently residing in the park is the mountain lion, which hunts primarily deer.

1989, a sow with three small cubs was seen in Green Gulch, and a second sow with cub may have been in the area as well.

However, there is no doubt that Big Bend is suitable bear habitat. At the time Vernon Bailey did his 1901 wildlife survey, black bears were common in the Chisos Mountains. Bailey commented that tracks and sign were abundant in all the upper canyons. Although black bears will eat meat, most of their diet consists of vegetable matter. Bailey reported that the Chisos Mountains black bears ate cactus fruits, acorns, juniper berries and pine nuts. Even in the late 1930s, bears still were reputed to be common in the Chisos Mountains, with Pine Canyon considered to be a particularly good area for bear sightings. It is suspected that unrestricted hunting combined with overgrazing—which eliminated many important bear foods—led to the bear's eventual extinction in Big Bend.

Another large predator that has been completely exterminated in the United States is the Mexican wolf. There may be a handful of animals still roaming the remote parts of Mexico, but most of the few remaining animals of this sub-species now are held in captivity as part of a proposed wolf reintroduction program. The Endangered Species Act requires the federal government to bring about the recovery of the species; however, this law presently is being ignored due mainly to opposition from ranchers near any proposed reintroduction site.

There is no doubt that wolves do on occasion eat livestock, just as mountain lions do. However, as with mountain lions, most wolves prefer natural prey to domestic animals. If prey populations are sufficiently high, losses of domestic livestock to wolves are low.

However, part of the responsibility for predation problems rests with the ranchers themselves. Instead of shepherding their animals, and corraling them at night to reduce predator opportunities, ranchers usually turn their animals out on the open range where they are completely vulnerable to predator attack. One can ask why the public should forgo reintroduction of native wildlife into a national park set aside and dedicated to preservation of *all* native species simply to reduce the operational costs of a few private ranchers. And while ranchers often demand, and get, taxpayer support for predator control, and even at times receive compensation for livestock losses to predators, the public is not compensated for its loss of native wildlife to view and enjoy. This includes the wolf.

Furthermore, given the small value of livestock and the limited amount of losses anticipated as a result of wolf predation, it very likely would cost taxpayers less to pay ranchers for livestock losses associated with wolf predation, rather than to pay for the captive breeding program.

At one time, Big Bend National Park supported a small resident wolf population. The combined area of the park, Black Gap Wildlife Area and the newly acquired Big Bend Ranch State Reserve collectively encompass more than a million acres, an area large enough to support a few wolf packs. Whether these are viable reintroduction sites will partially hinge on the willingness of Texans to accept wolves in these two areas. As of this writing, various proposals have been put forth for reintroduction and control methods.

Cold-blooded creatures

Although Big Bend is a desert park with limited water, it is nevertheless home to 34 species of fish that live primarily in the Rio Grande River or its tributaries. Two permanent streams flow through the park—Terlingua and Tornillo creeks. At one time surface water was more abundant in Big Bend, but like so many other resources, it was greatly reduced by livestock grazing, which eliminated the grassland cover and trampled the soils, decreasing the land's ability to absorb water. Rapid runoff led to channel scouring and down-cutting. As a consequence, many springs dried up and the flows of the larger streams were reduced to mere trickles.

Today, creeks like Terlingua and Tornillo are little more than a foot deep and can be crossed with a good running jump. It's hard to imagine that they could hold any fish at all. Yet there are a number of species unique to these drainages and the nearby Rio Grande, like the Mexican stoneroller and Chihuahua shiner—both threatened with extinction. These fish, along with several other species, use these small streams for spawning and nurseries. However, it appears no species uses them throughout the year. In the larger Rio Grande swim game fish like the channel, blue and flathead catfish.

The Mexican stoneroller and Chihuahua shiner mentioned above are considered threatened species, but they are not the rarest fish in the park. That dubious distinction goes to the tiny Big Bend gambusia found in a small spring near Rio Grande Village. It is found nowhere else in the world.

The fish was nearly eliminated when the common mosquitofish, an ecologically close relative, was introduced into the spring by the Park Service. Within two years, the more aggressive newcomer had nearly eliminated the native fish. At one point, there were only three Big Bend gambusia known to exist in the entire world. Fortunately, these were bred. After the common mosquitofish were poisoned, the natives were released back into the wild.

Ten amphibian and 61 reptile species live in Big Bend National Park. Since these animals are cold-

Right: Black-tailed rattlesnake.

Facing page, top: Whitetail deer keep to brushy terrains with good water supplies.
Bottom: Once found throughout the Southwest, including Big Bend, the Mexican wolf was trapped, shot and poisoned almost to extinction. Today perhaps 50 remain wild in Mexico and a few others are captive in U.S. zoos awaiting reintroduction into the wild.

blooded, they usually are not active during the colder months when most visitors are in the park, nor are they likely to be out during the heat of a summer day. As a consequence, it's possible to spend weeks or even months in Big Bend without seeing one live specimen.

Amphibians, just a notch above fish on the evolutionary scale, are dependent upon a watery habitat at some stage of their lives. Most toads and frogs, for example, depend upon water for reproduction—the tadpole stage. For this reason, most amphibians are closely associated with standing water. The Rio Grande leopard frog, for instance, is nearly always found immediately adjacent to a spring or creek.

In addition, adult toads and frogs do not drink but must absorb water through their skins. In the dry desert, this can be quite a trick. The red-spotted toad has a special patch of skin which is very thin to increase water absorption rates. After a summer rain, the red spotted toad will sometimes be found flattened against wet rocks trying to rehydrate.

Some amphibians have evolved with even more complex adaptations to desert existence. The Couch's spadefoot and western spadefoot toads are both reported to be in the park. They derive their names from a hard appendage on each foot, used for digging. Since water is scarce in the desert, the spadefoot avoids dehydration by digging itself a burrow and then slowly forming a self-sealing cocoon that prevents desiccation. The toad may remain encased for as long as 10 months. Spadefoot toads have the ability to reabsorb water from their bladders to keep from drying out. The urine is then expelled as urea when the toad leaves its burrow.

After a heavy summer rain the toad emerges to breed. In pools of water, females lay eggs that the males then fertilize. Because rain pools are ephemeral at best in the desert, after fertilization the toad's eggs develop and hatch very rapidly. In some species of spadefoot toad, this may be less than 12 hours. The resulting tadpoles can mature in 10 days.

The major evolutionary adaptation of reptiles was the ability to divorce themselves from direct dependence on water. They lay eggs in shells or, in a few species, bear live young. In addition, they do not lose moisture through their dry scaly skins and thus can venture onto dry land. It is not surprising, therefore, that Big Bend has six times more reptile species than amphibian species.

Reptiles are considered cold-blooded animals; however, this does not mean that they have no control over their body temperatures. Although reptiles have more toleration for a changing internal temperature compared to mammals, nevertheless they have definite body temperature zones. To maintain these ideal temperatures, reptiles make many behavior adjustments. For example, Big Bend's round-tailed horned lizard can flatten its body to expose a larger absorptive surface to the sun on cold days. Conversely, if too hot, the lizard pulls in its sides and becomes more cylindrical, thereby reducing its surface area. The lizard also will orient itself to the sun, turning broadside to warm up and facing the sun to narrow its exposure if too hot.

Snakes are even less tolerant of overheating than lizards. During the warmer months, many snakes are nocturnal or at least come out only in the cooler evening or early morning hours, hiding in burrows or rock crevices during the heat of the day. Conversely, in the colder weather they often hibernate or are active only for short periods of the day.

Facing page: A catfish from the Rio Grande.

ENDANGERED, THREATENED & PERIPHERAL SPECIES IN BIG BEND

A Mexican wolf in captivity.

Birds
Common Black Hawk (Threatened)
Gray Hawk (Threatened)
Zone-tailed Hawk (Threatened)
Peregrine Falcon (Endangered)
Bald Eagle (Endangered, peripheral)*
Black-capped Vireo (Endangered)

Mammals
Black bear (Endangered) *(Listed by Texas but not USWS)*
Mexican wolf (Endangered—no longer present)
Jaguarundi (Endangered—peripheral)
Ocelot (Endangered—peripheral)
Spotted bat (Threatened)
Mexican Long-nosed Bat (Endangered)

Fish
Big Bend Mosquitofish (Endangered)
Chihuahua Shiner (Threatened)
Mexican Stoneroller (Threatened)

Reptiles
Big Bend Gecko (Threatened)
Texas Horned Lizard (Threatened)
Texas Lyre Snake (Threatened)

• Present in areas peripheral to Big Bend National Park.

Presently Listed by the U.S. Fish and Wildlife Service and the Texas Parks and Wildlife Department. List adapted from El Paisano, *published by the Big Bend Natural History Association*

CHALLENGES AND CHANGES

Above: Burros at Lajitas Trading Post.

Facing page: Native cottonwood trees nearly became extinct in Big Bend because of seedling over-grazing; here, a few survivors along Terlingua Creek.

Big Bend is a designated World Biosphere Reserve. As such, it is to preserve a representation of a major world ecosystem—in this case the Chihuahuan Desert. But as is becoming increasingly apparent, no park is completely insulated from the problems of the modern world. No man is an island, and neither is a park. Both Big Bend's history and present conditions will dictate how successful park management is at preserving and, in some cases, even re-creating, a natural, wild landscape complete with a full complement of native flora and fauna.

Part of the problem stems from the artificial concept of borders. Many natural as well as unnatural processes fail to respect political boundaries drawn on a map. For example, although Big Bend is a designated Class 1 air-quality area and lies very far from any major pollution source, long-term monitoring has demonstrated that the air over Big Bend is not as clean as it once was. Visibility is less than 12 miles on three days of the year, while on the average of six days a year, visibility ranges up to 236 miles.

The wind that carries air pollutants to the park also can carry exotic seeds. Or non-native plants can also be introduced more directly—such as the non-native Rio Grande cottonwoods planted at Rio Grande Village and at Castolon. The Rio Grande also ferries the seeds of non-native plants. The tamarisk, now one of the most prevalent trees of the riparian zone, is an exotic that more than likely floated into the park on the river's current. At present more than 53 non-native plant species are known to occur in Big Bend and some, such as the tamarisk, have crowded out more desirable native species.

Non-native fauna is a problem as well. Animals can arrive like plants on the wind, or by floating down the river, or by merely walking into the park. For example, carp, a non-native fish species, now is abundant in the Rio Grande. The Barbary sheep, an animal introduced on nearby ranches as a game species, is now feral, and occasionally individuals wander into the park. As yet, we know of no breeding populations to have been established, though.

Not only does the wind bear poisoned and polluted air, but the Rio Grande is no longer clean, nor a naturally flowing river. Upstream agriculture is responsible for washing tons of pesticides and fertilizers into the river each year. In addition, dams on the Rio Grande in New Mexico have all but eliminated its flow below El Paso. The Rio Conchos, which flows out of Mexico, is the actual source of water for the river flowing through Big Bend. Even the Rio Conchos is regulated by three different dams, so that normal flood and low-water periods no longer occur.

But not all the problems come from outside the park. As in most national parks, the overall management emphasis has been on cosmetics and law enforcement,

instead of research and action to preserve the ecological health of these special places. Due to priorities set by the Reagan Administration, management direction recently was skewed even further in this direction. In most parks, far more is spent keeping the bathrooms painted than on researching ecosystems. Out of the 14,000 permanent employees in the National Park Service, only 75 are biologists. Even a major national park like Big Bend does not have a permanent biologist. In the absence of trained and paid full-time biological staff, often there is no one to coordinate long-term studies. Instead, most of the research falls to outside university researchers and many part-time rangers, volunteers and park-resource generalists who heroically strive to inventory and study our national treasures.

Ironically, because of the emphasis on construction and maintenance of facilities, the natural attributes originally responsible for the establishment of so many parks suffer neglect. Structures can be rebuilt. But if a species becomes extinct or we lose a major ecological process, we will not be able to bring it back again.

In the case of Big Bend, the park suffered tremendous degradation due to livestock grazing prior to its establishment. Much could be done to hasten recovery from this past abuse, but at present funding is limited by the aforementioned priorities.

Such a statement may come as a shock to most people visiting the park, since the scenery appears untouched. Nevertheless, grazing by domestic livestock has left a lasting mark on the park's flora and fauna. The damage may take centuries to heal. Fortunately, except for the continual ruination of the riparian zone by trespass livestock along the Rio Grande, Big Bend is slowly recovering from the impacts of the ranching era. In the moister, higher elevations of the park, many plant communities have made remarkable recoveries from the years of range abuse. But in the lower, drier zones, it may take many more decades before full recovery occurs.

Some indicators of range abuse include the overabundance of cactus, creosote bush and other plants livestock find unpalatable. The deep arroyos, dried-up springs and severely channelized waterways also result from past range abuse. However, it would be incorrect to assume that, prior to livestock grazing, desert plants were absent from the park, that arroyos formed only after grazing began and that desert pavement suddenly appeared when the first cow chomped on the native grasses. All these elements existed prior to the ranching era. Nevertheless, after widespread livestock grazing was initiated in the 1880s, they greatly expanded their influence and impact.

It is important to note that livestock grazing does not necessarily result in range abuse. In the humid East or even on the Great Plains where grasslands were heavily grazed by bison and other large mammals, the ecosystems are very tolerant of grazing pressure. However, the desert grasslands in Big Bend and many other areas of the West evolved with no large-mammal grazing. These ecosystems simply cannot tolerate significant cropping.

Even though Big Bend is extremely dry and rather unproductive, it is important to realize that it was a less

---

Right: *Eroded gully near Sawmill Mountain along the upper portion of Terlingua Creek. The rate of arroyo cutting and gullying increased dramatically after the introduction of livestock into the region.*

Facing page, top: *Impacts from livestock grazing include soil erosion, loss of vegetation and competition with native wildlife. The plants in this picture are endangered as erosion wastes away the soil around them. Normally, vegetative cover would prevent such erosion.*
Bottom: *The single largest problem facing Big Bend is the past and continuing damage to the park's ecological health as a result of domestic livestock grazing. Even though grazing has been officially banned within the park since 1944, animals from Mexico, as well as occasionally from surrounding ranches, stray across the park's borders.*

harsh-looking place a hundred or more years ago. For example, Terlingua Creek, which enters the Rio Grande by the mouth of Santa Elena Canyon, is now a wide sandy desert wash, barely flowing most of the year and nearly devoid of trees. Yet when Lieutenant William Echols led his camel expeditions through Big Bend in 1859 and 1860, he reported finding grass stirrup-high along Terlingua Creek. And James Gillett, foreman of the G-4 Ranch—one of the early ranch operations on Terlingua Creek—described it as a "bold running stream, studded with cottonwood timber and alive with beaver" in 1885 when the ranch first began operations in the area. Tobosa grass hay was harvested at the turn of the century on Tornillo Flat, visible along the road between Panther Junction and Persimmon Gap, while today this area is an eroded barren "desert" area dominated by creosote bush.

Most historical accounts of Big Bend blame a three-year period of unrestricted grazing just prior to the establishment of the park for the documented overgrazed condition of the land. According to Roland Wauer, in his book *Naturalist's Big Bend* there were an estimated 3,880 cattle, 25,700 goats, 9,000 sheep and 310 horses grazing in Big Bend at the time of the 1942 land purchases. But, by 1945, there were 19,000 to 25,000 cattle (still fewer than the G-4 ran on its holdings in 1891), 6,000 to 8,000 sheep, 15,000 to 18,000 goats and 1,000 horses. There is no doubt that such numbers had a severe impact on Big Bend's rangelands. However, these three years of extreme overgrazing did not mark the beginning of range abuse. The intentional overstocking was rather the *coup de grace*, laid on an already badly overgrazed and abused landscape.

There are many early accounts that suggest overgrazing was widespread in Big Bend long before the final three years of open grazing. In his book, the *Homesteaders' Story*, J.O. Langford described Tornillo Flat at the turn of the century as a fertile valley with waist-high grasses. At that time, antelope were abundant. Overgrazing changed Tornillo Flat into a badland of eroded gullies, creosote flats and desert pavement. Gone with the grass and soil are the large groups of antelope; fewer than a dozen individuals frequent the area today.

Another piece of evidence that suggests long-term range abuse is simply the large number of cattle reportedly run on Big Bend ranges. For example, the G-4 Ranch that covered the western portion of what is now Big Bend National Park owned 6,000 cattle in 1885, but by 1891 ran an estimated 30,000 head. These were only a small portion of the animals grazing Big Bend rangelands. An estimated 60,000 cattle were rounded up in Big Bend during 1886 alone! And this was before area herds had grown to their maximum sizes. On these fragile desert grasslands, such large numbers could not be, and in fact were not, sustained. But before reduction took place, tremendous ecological damage had occurred.

A report entitled *Mammals of the Big Bend Area of Texas,* published by the University of California in 1942, lists the results of a 1930s wildlife survey in what was then the proposed Big Bend National Park. It repeatedly describes the impacts of grazing *prior* to the park's establishment and the overgrazing that supposedly occurred only from 1942 to 1944. For example, when discussing the loss of black bears from the Chisos Mountains, the authors state that "heavy grazing by domestic stock probably has reduced the bear's food supply and protective cover." Mentioning the very small number of javelina found in the park during their 1930s survey, the authors conclude that "heavy grazing by domestic stock has greatly reduced forage and shelter and probably has been an important factor in reducing the range and number of javelinas." Likewise the antelope: "the lower country in the park area has been severely overgrazed and is not now suitable for the introduction of antelope." Finally, the bighorn sheep:

"the former range of the bighorn has been heavily grazed by domestic sheep and goats."

Although many plant communities in the park, particularly at the moister, higher elevations, have recovered quite well since the 1940s, trespass livestock from Mexico are still a major problem here. This illegal grazing continues to degrade the park's most important habitat—the riparian zone.

The problem of trespass livestock is not a recent phenomenon. Letters written by park officials and conservationists, dating from the early 1970s, discuss the problem of livestock grazing in detail. During my first float trip on the Rio Grande in 1974, I saw dozens of trespass animals along the river and on each subsequent float, including one in 1989, I saw no lessening of the numbers. Nearly 20 years of discussion has provided little amelioration of the problem.

One consequence of past and present livestock grazing is the near-extinction of the narrow-leaf cottonwood from riparian areas. At one time, this species was abundant along the Rio Grande flood plain and on tributaries like Terlingua Creek. Despite the cottonwood's ability to sprout vigorously if the tree is cut down by beavers or even humans, the dramatic reduction in native cottonwood suggests that years of repeated browsing of seedlings and sprouts resulted in its near-elimination from park flora.

How does the loss of cottonwood affect the park's biological integrity? Cottonwoods are the only Rio Grande riparian tree species that attains large dimensions. Such trees have a distinct ecological function, including providing suitable habitat for cavity-nesting

Right: The nearby Big Bend Ranch State Park includes the Bofecillos Mountains, volcanic in origin.

Facing page, top: Viewing the Sierra Quemada from the South Rim of the Chisos Mountains.
Bottom: A park naturalist explains Big Bend geology to visitors.

birds like the golden fronted woodpecker; their large canopies also serve as platforms for nesting birds like hawks. And when the old trees die and fall into streams, they act as channel stabilizers and thereby protect fish habitat. Finally, humans simply enjoy the shade and greenery that large cottonwoods bring to the otherwise harsh desert landscape. All of these values have been compromised severely or lost, as a result of livestock grazing.

Admittedly, solutions are difficult. It would be undesirable and probably impossible to fence the entire park boundary. At present the Park Service occasionally rounds up some of the trespass stock and ships it to Presidio, forcing owners to travel some distance to claim their animals. However, this is a time-consuming and costly procedure for the park. Nevertheless, live-stock grazing has far more ecological impact on the park than someone camping in an illegal site or a few pieces of litter in the campgrounds. If the park administration really would like to emphasize livestock control, a few people who presently pick up litter, paint bathrooms and hand out back-country permits—all of which deal primarily with minor impacts to the park's surface appearance—should be shifted to rounding up the trespass livestock.

Livestock grazing was detrimental to more than the plant communities and large mammals. Many desert streams, such as Terlingua Creek and Tornillo Creek, are inhabited by fish found nowhere else in the world. The erosion and subsequent depletion of the water table as a consequence of livestock grazing had serious consequences for native fish, along with other water-dependent wildlife such as turtles and amphibians.

Even the fabulous bird watching for which Big Bend is renowned has been affected by past and present livestock grazing. Studies have shown that 75 to 80 of the species in desert regions are partially or wholly dependent upon riparian zones for their survival. Any destruction of these wetlands brings about a reduction in all species associated with that particular habitat. Cattle, in particular, tend to congregate in riparian zones where they trample vegetation, break down banks, and eat the vegetation. Many of the songbirds one might see in Big Bend would be much more common were it not for the general decline in riparian zones throughout the park—and the West as a whole.

The loss of nesting birds in this riparian zone, of course, affects more than bird watchers. At least one falcon researcher believes that continued overgrazing of the floodplain zone, particularly on the Mexican side of the river, is reducing the prey base for the endangered peregrine falcon.

A few birds that formerly inhabited the park, like the Montezuma quail, were driven to local extinction by severe overgrazing of their grassland habitats. The Montezuma quail was reintroduced into Big Bend in 1973, but recovery appears to have failed.

While still biologically rich, Big Bend is nonetheless a depauperate ecosystem, due in large part to livestock grazing. Grassland communities, native cottonwoods, and animals from fish to bighorn sheep to wolves and bears have been diminished or eliminated. Until trespass livestock are eliminated from the Rio Grande, until bighorn are seen again seen on Mariscal Mountain, until Terlingua Creek is once again a "bold running stream with beaver and cottonwood," and until wolves are once again heard howling in the Chisos, Big Bend will not truly be a Biosphere Reserve.

Right: *View from the South Rim, looking through a wind-twisted piñon.*

Facing page: *Tornillo Flat. Early settlers described this area as grass-covered, where they saw many antelope. At one time, native hay was harvested here, but overgrazing eliminated the grass cover and the creosote bush moved in. Erosion has stripped away top soil and, even with recovery efforts, it probably will take hundreds of years before Tornillo Flat once again is a grassy basin.*

GUIDE TO THE BIG BEND REGION

Above: Brittlebrush.

Facing page, top: Backpackers in the Chisos Mountains.
Bottom: Kayaking the Rio Grande.

Alpine—A community located by the Davis Mountains approximately 100 miles from the park. Originally named Murphyville, this town was established when the Southern Pacific Railroad arrived in 1882. Now a retirement center and home to Sul Ross University.

Basin—A mountain-encircled valley high in the Chisos Mountains that once was used as an Apache hide-out, then as pastures for livestock, as a CCC camp during the 1930s and, presently, as the location of a lodge, campground and other facilities. Many hiking trails radiate out from this area.

Big Bend Ranch State Natural Area—The state of Texas recently acquired 215,000 acres of the former Big Bend Ranch located along the Rio Grande River between Lajitas and Presidio. The park includes Colorado Canyon on the Rio Grande; the Solitario, a circular eight-mile uplift; the volcanic Bofecillos Mountains; and Alamito Creek. This is the largest state holding in Texas.

Boquillas—A small Mexican village across the Rio Grande from Rio Grande Village. Visitors can cross to it by ferry. At one time, there was also a Boquillas, Texas near the present site of Rio Grande Village, which included a post office and store.

Boquillas Canyon—Longest of the three major canyons within the park and yet the easiest to float. Here the Rio Grande cuts through the towering Sierra Del Carmen Mountains.

Castolon—Originally a small farming community and store. During the Mexican Revolution, an army unit was stationed here. The fort is restored and the old barracks are operated as a store. Cotton was grown along the floodplain, including the area where the Cottonwood Campground now sits. These fields are now covered largely by mesquite.

Comanche Trail—A major Indian pathway into Mexico used by raiding parties of Comanche and Apache Indians. One prong of the trail passed through what is now Big Bend National Park, through Persimmon Gap and down Tornillo Creek. An alternative route followed what is now Route 118 and crossed into Mexico at Lajitas.

Dagger Flats—An area near the base of the Dead Horse Mountains off Highway 385 between Panther Junction and Marathon, known for its stands of giant dagger, a large yucca whose U.S. distribution is limited to the Big Bend region.

Deadhorse Mountains—Located east of the old Ore Road, the Deadhorse Mountains are the northern extension of the Sierra Del Carmen Range of Mexico. These mountains are lower than the Chisos Mountains and consequently more desert-like in aspect.

Elephant Tusk Peak—A prominent peak of volcanic origins in the Sierra Quemada which, due to its isolation, appears to some people to resemble the tusk of an elephant.

Emory Peak—Named for William Emory, Chief Surveyor of the U.S.-Mexican border in 1850. Located in the Chisos Mountains, at 7,835 feet, it is the third-highest peak in Texas and the highest mountain in Big Bend National Park.

Ernst Tinaja—A natural water-filled rock basin carved by erosion into the limestones of the Deadhorse Mountains. Tinajas are important sources of water for wildlife.

Glenn Springs—A large spring and oasis nine miles west on a dirt road from the Panther Junction-Rio Grande Village road. Named for W.J. Glenn, who surveyed the area in 1881. This was the site of a major candelilla wax factory in 1914 and an army outpost during the Mexican Revolution. In 1916, bandits raided this settlement.

Grapevine Hills—Low hills of granite boulders located

north of the Chisos Mountains. Considered a laccolith, formed when magma was intruded into a pocket in the bedrock. The magma subsequently hardened into granite. Later the overlying rock layers eroded, exposing the granite to view.

Hot Springs—Natural hot springs along the Rio Grande River near the mouth of Tornillo Creek, which were developed by J.O. Langford as a health resort and store shortly after the turn of the century. Historic ruins as well as an old hot spring bath still exist.

Johnson Ranch—Located along the Rio Grande between Castolon and Rio Grande Village, this combination ranch, trading post and air strip was occupied until the 1940s.

Luna's Jacal—A jacal is a primitive shelter. These ruins, which lie along the road between Santa Elena Canyon and Maverick once belonged to Mexican settler Gilberto Luna. Luna is reputed to have lived to 108 years of age.

Marathon—Small gateway community to Big Bend National Park located on junction of Highway 90 and 385. Home of the historic Gage Hotel.

Marfa—Originally a railhead on the Southern Pacific tracks, later a major supply point for mines at Schafter and nearby ranches. Now a community of 2,500 people.

Mariscal Mine—Located on the northern edge of Mariscal Mountain. Quicksilver (mercury) was discovered here in 1900 but the mine operated during the 1920s. Another attempt at mining occurred during the 1940s, but the mine since has passed into Park Service ownership.

Paint Gap Hills—Low hills formed when volcanic magma was intruded into existing bedrock and subsequently hardened in place. Later erosion stripped away the overlying rock, exposing the harder rock that now makes up these hills.

Panther Junction—Location of park headquarters, visitor center and post office.

Presidio—Community on the Rio Grande northwest of Big Bend National Park. Originally the location of several Pueblo Indian villages, later site of a Spanish military fort. For centuries it has been a major entranceway into Mexico.

Punta la Sierra—Literally the point of the mountains. The southernmost portion of the Chisos Mountains.

Rio Grande Village—Once part of a farm, now a campground, picnic area and store.

Rosillos Mountains—A small range just east of Highway 385 and north of the park boundary. Part of this range recently was acquired by the Park Service in the Harte Ranch purchase that adds 67,000 acres to the park.

Sam Nail Place—Remains of old ranch built by Sam Nail in 1916. Located off the Ross Maxwell Drive. Good bird watching area.

Santa Elena Canyon—Located downstream from Lajitas, this is the narrowest of the major Rio Grande Canyons. Here the Rio Grande has cut through the limestone uplift of the Mesa de Anguila. One rapid, Rockslide, is a major hazard for boaters.

Sierra Del Carmen—Massive mountain range in Mexico just across the Rio Grande from Rio Grande Village, composed primarily of limestone. The highest peaks are more than a thousand feet higher than the Chisos Mountains.

Sierra Quemada—A lower portion of the Chisos Mountains below the South Rim, including such peaks as Elephant Tusk and Mule Ear Peaks.

Study Butte—Once the center of quicksilver mining effort, now a growing retirement community and tourist gateway facility for the park.

Terlingua Creek—A major perennial stream that reaches the Rio Grande near the mouth of Santa Elena Canyon.

Terlingua Abaja—An old Mexican settlement along the lower portion of Terlingua Creek near the mouth of Santa Elena Canyon. The adobe walls of this village are still visible.

Vernon Bailey Mountain—A major peak in the Chisos Mountain Basin named for an early biologist, Vernon Bailey.

The Window—A slot in the mountains of the Chisos Mountains Basin. The most popular trail in the park winds from the Basin Campground to the Window and back.

Overleaf: *The Window in the Chisos Mountains at sunset.*